WALKING

—

CALDERDALE

Paul Hannon

—

Hillside

HILLSIDE
PUBLICATIONS
20 Wheathead Crescent
Keighley
West Yorkshire
BD22 6LX

First published 1989
Fully Revised 3rd edition 2010

ISBN 978-1-907626-07-4

Cover illustration: Eaves Wood, Colden Clough, Heptonstall
Back cover: Pecket Well; Hebden Bridge; Crimsworth Dean
Page One: The Bride Stones, above Todmorden
Page Three: Sundial at Baitings
(Paul Hannon/Hillslides Picture Library)

The sketch maps in this book are based upon
1947 Ordnance Survey One-Inch maps
and earlier Six-Inch maps

Printed in Great Britain by
Carnmor Print
95-97 London Road
Preston
Lancashire
PR1 4BA

CONTENTS

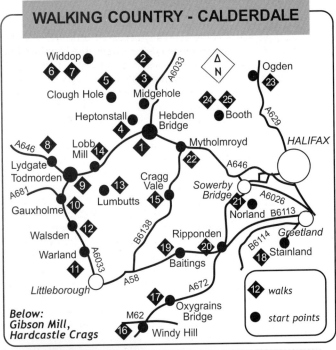

WALKING COUNTRY - CALDERDALE

Widdop

6 7

5

Clough Hole

2

3

A6033

N

Ogden

23

24 25

Booth

A629

Midgehole

Heptonstall

4

Hebden Bridge

HALIFAX

A646

8

Lobb Mill

14

1

Mytholmroyd

22

A646

Lydgate

Todmorden

9

13

Cragg Vale

Sowerby Bridge

A6026

A681

Lumbutts

15

21

Norland B6113

Gauxholme

10

Walsden

12

B6138

Ripponden

B6114

Greetland

Warland

A6033

19

20

18

Stainland

11

Baitings

Littleborough

A58

A672

17

Oxygrains Bridge

Below:
Gibson Mill,
Hardcastle Crags

M62

16

Windy Hill

12 *walks*

• *start points*

6

INTRODUCTION

South Pennines is the generally accepted term for describing that part of the Pennine range lying between the Yorkshire Dales and the Peak District, and the area explored within these pages constitutes the heart of this region, the upper valley of Yorkshire's River Calder. This well-defined geographical unit sees moorland watersheds with neighbouring valleys in Yorkshire and Lancashire being the limit of exploration: only to the east, where the Calder leaves the high country for the larger towns, must an arbitrary line be drawn. Since 1974 the title 'Calderdale' has been put to use in local government, with whose patch we coincide apart from the aforementioned lower third of the district, where the conurbations of Halifax, Sowerby Bridge, Brighouse and Elland are found.

This guide commences at the 'gateway' of Sowerby Bridge, where the rivers Calder and Ryburn merge. Upstream the Ryburn Valley strikes southwards to Ripponden and the moors, while the main valley heads west to the upper dale's two towns of Hebden Bridge and Todmorden. On the way it absorbs major side valleys carved out by Luddenden Brook, Cragg Brook, Hebden Water and Walsden Water. The larger settlements squeeze into the cramped valley floor, shared with river, canal, road and railway. Steep flanks rise to intervening ledges where older villages, predecessors of their bigger brothers below, almost shake hands across the deep divides. Higher still, rough pasture gives way to open moorland, where the mill chimney 2 miles away might as well be 200 miles distant. Calderdale's fascination is its unique blend of town and country: the two are inextricably linked, and once one accepts the less appealing aspects of industrial demands, then one can revel in a feast of fascinating walking country.

Many features of this district's industrial past, in particular, provide a great deal of interest to the observant walker. The hills hereabouts are laced with a network of centuries-old trade routes used mainly by packhorses: many of these escaped 'improvement', and numerous sections of stone causeway have survived, laying virtually dormant in wait for today's foot-traveller to bring them back to life, albeit for a new purpose. Hugging the valley bottom, in contrast, is the Rochdale Canal, which largely replaced the pack-horse routes and whose colourful towpath now provides miles of uninterrupted leisurely walking.

Tumbling to the floor of the upper dale at regular intervals are short-lived but deep-cut and richly wooded little valleys: these are cloughs, where some of the earliest mills were built in the most unlikely settings. Up on the tops one is never far from a reservoir, the earlier ones made to serve the canal, others to slake the ever-growing thirsts of the expanding towns down the valley. This is solid gritstone country, and sharing the higher ground with the reservoirs are numerous clusters of boulders and crags, with the weathered natural outcrops outshining the countless sites of former quarries. Mainly small-scale operations known as delphs, they provided the material for the drystone walls, reservoirs and buildings throughout the dale. Interestingly enough the River Calder, underlying theme of these walks, is seen only infrequently. Occasional spells by the canal do give rare opportunities to encounter it, but by accident rather than design. No, Calderdale's walking is not in the valley bottom, it is to be found on the hillsides and bracing tops of this characterful upland.

A welcome aspect of walking in this well-populated district is the availability of public transport. Almost all the starting points are served by buses, while a good rail service patrols the valley bottom. Such is the compactness of the area that over half of the walks are within a couple of miles of a station. The generally good waymarking and condition of the paths is an indication of the local authority's commendable valuation of its outstanding path network. In your travels you encounter the Pennine Way, which crosses the area from Blackstone Edge in the south to Walshaw Dean in the north; and the 50-mile Calderdale Way, which encircles the district. The latter is a splendid example of what can be achieved in an 'unfashionable' area: this you encounter on numerous occasions.

Access to the countryside

The vast majority of walks in this guide are on public rights of way with no access restrictions. While the implementation of Right to Roam in 2004 brought new freedoms to walk responsibly over these vast swathes of wonderful landscapes, the walks within these pages, whilst often incorporating sections of Open Access, do in fact tread only rights of way or pre-existing permissive paths: such walks are noted in their introduction. Open Access does however give scope for more variation to your chosen route. Of various restrictions the two most notable are that dogs are normally banned from grouse moors; and also that the areas can be closed to walkers for up to 28 days each year, subject to advance notice being given. Inevitably the most likely times will be from the 'Glorious Twelfth', the start of the grouse shooting season in August. Further information can be obtained from the helpline listed below, and ideally from information centres. Finally, bear in mind that in springtime, avoiding tramping over open country away from paths and tracks would help to safeguard the most crucial period for vulnerable ground-nesting birds.

Using the guide
Each walk is self contained, with essential information being followed by a concise route description and simple map. Dovetailed in between are notes and illustrations of features along the way. Snippets of information have been placed in *italics* to ensure that the essential route description is easier to locate. The sketch maps serve to identify the location of the routes rather than the fine detail, and whilst the description should be sufficient to guide you around, an Ordnance Survey map is strongly recommended.

To gain the most from a walk, the detail of the 1:25,000 scale Explorer map is unsurpassed. It also gives the option to vary walks as desired, giving an improved picture of your surroundings and the availability of linking paths. One essential map covers all of the walks in this book:

• *Explorer OL21 - South Pennines*

Also useful for planning are Landranger maps 103, 104, 109, 110.

USEFUL ADDRESSES

Calderdale Countryside & Forestry Unit
Wesley Court, Crossley Street, Halifax HX1 1UJ • 01422-393214

Information Centres
Visitor & Canal Centre **Hebden Bridge** HX7 8AF • 01422-843831
15 Burnley Road **Todmorden** OL14 7BU • 01706-818181
The Piece Hall **Halifax** HX1 1RE • 01422-368725

Open Access
Helpline • 0845-100 3298 *or* www.countrysideaccess.gov.uk

Public Transport Information
MetroLine • 0113 245 7676 *or* www.wymetro.com

EDGE END MOOR

START Hebden Bridge   Grid ref. SD 991272

DISTANCE $5^{1}2$ miles (9km)

ORDNANCE SURVEY MAPS
1:50,000
Landranger 103 - Blackburn & Burnley
1:25,000
Explorer OL21 - South Pennines

ACCESS Start from the town centre. Ample car parks. Served by Halifax-Todmorden bus and train.

Woodlands sandwich a bright stroll on a shelf high above the valley, encircling Edge End Moor in the shadow of Stoodley Pike

'South Pennine Centre' Hebden Bridge is very much the focal point for this set of walks. It is for here that most visitors make, partly for its position at the foot of Hebden Dale (universally known as Hardcastle Crags), but also for its own attractions. Its houses climb alarmingly up steep hillsides above the meeting of the valleys, while in and around the vibrant centre are canal trips, excellent shops, pubs, cafes and an invaluable visitor centre. The town featured prominently on the trans-Pennine packhorse routes, and the bridge over Hebden Water dates from the 16th century. It developed greatly with the fast-flowing streams ideal for powering flourishing textile mills as the industrial revolution took hold, and canals, then railways forged through the valley. In the second half of the 20th century its inexpensive housing and 'backwater' status brought an influx of 'hippy'-style residents, and the buzzing little town happily retains countless quirky elements and corners.

From the visitor centre head briefly left along the main road, then turn left on Holme Street to gain the canal towpath at a stone-arched bridge at Blackpit Lock. Cross and turn right along the other bank. *At once you are carried over the River Calder by the Black Pit Aqueduct of 1797.* The path quickly turns off, up some steps then along to the right to meet a road. Go left here, through the novelty of pedestrian lights on the railway bridge and up. Almost at once turn right up an access road rising away. It runs left behind a row of houses, but soon leave by a more inviting walled green path doubling back up to the right. *As height is gained you savour possibly the finest bird's-eye view of the town, with the wooded Colden and Hebden valleys striking away behind.* At a wall, with a house just beyond, turn left on a much vaguer path rising steeply into Crow Nest Wood. At the top a stile empties onto a broad rough lane, with a mast just to the left. Cross straight over and up the fieldsides, soon reaching the brow whereupon virtually all the climbing is already done. Ahead, Stoodley Pike appears.

This course is mantained along several fieldsides, past a farm and becoming a grass track to meet an access road at the end. Cross straight over and along the super walled green way of Pinnacle Lane. *Pinnacle Farm is quickly passed,*

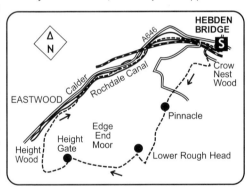

an attractive and enviably sited house with mullioned windows, dating from the 17th century. Just keep straight on this aptly-named lane with the Stoodley Pike monument directly ahead. *Sections of stone causey occupy a short length, appropriately at a moist section.* Eventually this green lane empties onto a rough farm lane. Turn right on this to Lower Rough Head Farm. Here enter a field on the left, where an old embanked green way follows the wall to a kissing-gate at the far end. Head directly away across briefly moist rough pasture, soon dropping rather more pleasantly to a stile in an old wall. Again head directly away, a nice little path dropping into scattered trees. At the bottom bear right above a wood and house, passing through a gate/stile at the end to join a grass track. Advance on this over the field to a gate into Height Gate.

Go left on the enclosed rough drive, passing Height Farm with its mullioned windows and quickly swinging sharp left. *The tall monument looms particularly highly above now.* As it drops away, leave by a more inviting old walled green way on the right, just as the left-hand wall ends. This drops down into trees and onto a cart track. Go briefly right to a hairpin bend, then enter the trees in front. A super path runs to the right beneath the wall and along the top of Burnt Acres Wood, an airy traverse high above a steep bank that opens out with great views down into the valley. This path runs an unfailing course along the bank top, over an intervening stile and above denser woodland to alight upon an enclosed green way. Turn left down this superb old access road all the way to the valley floor. Joining a modern access road at the bottom, drop left to a canal bridge. Cross and double back beneath it to return unfailingly to the start. *En route you pass several locks and an 'island' spell as the river comes in on your left: steep woodland hangs above the canal. Almost at the end is the inviting Stubbing Wharf pub.*

The old bridge, Hebden Bridge

HARDCASTLE CRAGS

START *Midgehole   Grid ref. SD 988291*

DISTANCE *5¹2 miles (9km)*

ORDNANCE SURVEY MAPS
1:50,000
Landranger 103 - Blackburn & Burnley
1:25,000
Explorer OL21 - South Pennines

ACCESS *Start from the National Trust car park at New Bridge, main car park for Hardcastle Crags, signposted off the Keighley road out of Hebden Bridge. Summer weekend bus from Hebden Bridge.*

> *Renowned woodlands, and a climb to old hilltop hamlets and gentle moor-edge tracks high above Crimsworth Dean*

Hardcastle Crags is the name by which everyone knows the valley of Hebden Dale, through which flows Hebden Water. The majority of this beautifully wooded, deep-cut dale is in the care of the National Trust, and draws crowds from far and wide. From the bottom car park head up the drive a few strides until just past a solitary lodge, then fork left on a path descending to Hebden Water. Here a wide beckside path is met, and this is accompanied upstream for almost a mile and a half to Gibson Mill, only straying from the bank to circumvent two short, impassable sections. After a splendid lengthy beckside spell you rise again (both options quickly merge) to run to a T-junction. Drop back to the beck at stepping-stones, from where the last stage is an unbroken stroll upstream to the mill. *Two further sets of stepping-stones are passed, giving options to trace the opposite bank for a short spell. A 'psalm-plaque' adorns a rock in the beck just before the final stepping-stones as the mill appears ahead.*

Gibson Mill was founded in 1800 as an early water-powered cotton mill: it ceased to operate in the 1890s, becoming an oddly-sited dance hall and even a roller-skating rink during the mid-20th century. The well-preserved building is an imposing sight in its wooded environs, and features a cafe, WCs, shop and information, as well as exhibitions. Related features include a row of workers' cottages, while a fine stone-arched bridge spans the beck. Around the back is a millpond. At Gibson Mill the drive is rejoined to climb above the beck, levelling out alongside the steep rise of Hardcastle Crags. These invite an ungainly scramble just up to the left. *This group of modest outcrops occupies a prominent knoll bedecked with clumps of heather, with a slender ridge rising well above the treetops. As a result this airy spot is a superb vantage point.*

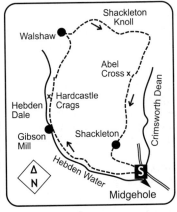

Continuing on from the crags, simply remain on the main drive which swings uphill to merge with a firmer access road at the top of the wood. *The first open views reveal the Gorple moors to the left, up-dale.* Go left for a few minutes to the hamlet of Walshaw. *This ancient and very attractive settlement features a shooting lodge to the left, whose impressive front boasts an enviable view down-dale.* Immediately before entering, however, your way turns off right, as a gate sends a walled track doubling back. This soon becomes unenclosed to cross to a tiny beck and a gate. It then rises round the top side of a much larger pasture, fading but remaining with the top wall almost to the far corner. Here a gate transfers you onto open moor, and a broad wallside path contours to the right beneath Shackleton Knoll. *At around 1214ft/370m the walk's highest point is reached: ubiquitous features of the view are Heptonstall church tower and Stoodley Pike.* As the environs of Crimsworth Dean are approached, the moor is vacated at a gate to descend a walled green track, Coppy Lane, to a junction at ruinous

Nook, once a house of substance. Turn right on a broader track along the flank of Crimsworth Dean. Remain on the track until just beyond a cattle-grid after the first farm buildings at Laithe, where a stile lurks in the low wall/fence on the right. Contour across the field to a grassy cart track, with Abel Cross just ahead. *This is in fact two identical shafts, thought to mark a medieval pack-route.*

Advance straight on the drive to the farm buildings at Abel Cote, preceded by several springs. Entering the yard, advance to a gate on the left after the house, and cross a field bottom to a gate at the end. A lengthy level section ensues, maintaining this contour above Crimsworth Dean. Continue to a stile at the very corner ahead, transferring to the left side of the wall. This easy line crosses several field tops, and at the last gate the hamlet of Shackleton appears just ahead. Cross to a wall that forms in the field centre, leading on to a stile in the very corner between buildings. Emerging onto the access road in the heart of the hamlet go briefly right, and just after the last building take a gate on the left.

The wooded gulf of Hebden Dale is now below you. Dropping away, a narrow, grassy way forms between old walls, dropping to a stile at the bottom back into the top of the woods. Firstly go a few strides right to emerge onto a gritstone crag, the walk's last great viewpoint. Back at the stile, take a path dropping left beneath the wall, within a minute reaching a path junction. Keep left, slanting down a splendid course on a substantially causeyed way. This drops at a good gradient through the wood, reaching the corner of a large open pasture. Keeping above this you quickly leave the trees to become pleasantly enclosed, and still largely on the old stone causey. At the bottom this empties you back into the wood, with the upper car park just below.

Abel Cross, Crimsworth Dean

3

CRIMSWORTH DEAN

START *Midgehole   Grid ref. SD 988291*

DISTANCE *5^{3}4 miles (9km)*

ORDNANCE SURVEY MAPS
1:50,000
Landranger 103 - Blackburn & Burnley
Landranger 104 - Leeds, Bradford & Harrogate
1:25,000
Explorer OL21 - South Pennines

ACCESS *Start from the National Trust car park at New Bridge, main car park for Hardcastle Crags, signposted off the Keighley road out of Hebden Bridge. Summer weekend bus from Hebden Bridge.*

> *After a stiff start, an easy walk ensues to combine superb woodland and beck scenery with a bracing moorland ramble*

Hardcastle Crags is the name by which everyone in the district fondly knows the valley of Hebden Dale, through which flows Hebden Water. The majority of this beautifully wooded, deep-cut dale is in the care of the National Trust, and attracts large crowds from far and wide. Offering refreshment just across New Bridge on Hebden Water is Midgehole Working Mens' Club, affectionately known as the Blue Pig. From the car park cross the bridge and take a narrow way climbing behind the WCs. Behind an early solitary house, ignore its drive slanting away and continue climbing on a stony track between crumbling walls. This superb old bridleway winds about effortlessly to gain height through the woodland of Pecket Well Clough, resplendent with beeches.

As height is gained the towering Wadsworth war memorial may be seen high to the left, and can be visited by branching off at some old steps where a narrow path rises steeply left. A stile *gives access to the small pasture containing the monument. This striking edifice is a remarkable tribute to the lost sons of the parish: perched above a colourful pocket of heather and gritstone it commands a glorious view, with Heptonstall church silhouetted and the environs of Hardcastle Crags as on a map.* The main path soon levels out to cross the clough before meeting a similar path to rise steeply left (all flagged) onto the A6033 at Pecket Well. *This old mill community sits high on the moor edge: the Robin Hood pub is just along to the left.* Cross straight over the Hebden Bridge-Keighley road and up a short-lived path onto a wide back road, turning right along it. *Massive views look over densely wooded Hebden Dale to Heptonstall and Stoodley Pike.*

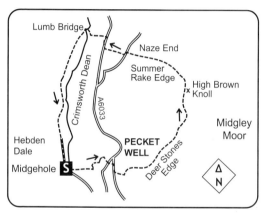

After a few minutes leave by surfaced Shaw Croft Hill up to the left. It ends at a short terrace of tiny cottages but a narrow, walled path escapes to the left. It rises through an open heathery area to soon join a hard access road at a junction: take the walled track rising directly away, ignoring two drives off and rising through a gate/stile onto open moorland. Opt for the broad track rising half-right, and within 100 yards double back left at a junction of like ways. The track quickly levels out: some way ahead you might spot the white Ordnance Survey column on High Brown Knoll, which is your objective. The track runs on to a wall corner, with a ruin and old ventilation shaft behind it. After a few yards with the wall it

17

turns to rise across the moor, forking into two distinct sunken ways: the right one is better used to rise grandly to a large cairn at Deer Stones Edge. *Denser grouse moors are alongside you now, while Ovenden Moor windfarm appears ahead.*

A good path runs northwards along this largely grassy edge, passing a few spoilheaps of old quarries. With the trig point now closer the path fades as the minor edge swings left: faced with a few reeds bear right away from the edge. Around a peatier area and through a line of simple butts, the way rises left bound for the trig. Alongside to the left is the sunken Limer's Gate, which bears off left. Remain on the grassy path which surmounts the final inviting slopes to gain the waiting Ordnance Survey column on High Brown Knoll. *At 1453ft/443m this is the summit of the walk. It stands a mere 25ft/8m below Nab Hill, 2 miles to the north-east and the highest point between the Keighley-Hebden Bridge and Keighley-Halifax roads. The extensive panorama is a distinctly moorland one, with Fly Flatts Reservoir visible beneath the wind turbines.*

Another path is met here: go left on it, quickly passing through an area of gritstone boulders. *From here to Lumb Bridge you follow with minor variations the route of the Limer's Gate, a centuries-old packhorse way along which lime would be transported from Lancashire to the farms of the Calder Valley.* The intermittently cairned path remains clear as it runs above the boulders of modest Summer Rake Edge to drop slightly onto the better stony edge of Naze End, with the A6033 just below. *Throughout this stage are massive views left over almost this entire area.* The path descends to a gate onto the road, going briefly left to a gate/stile on the right. A path drops down a reedy pasture, with the deep valley of Crimsworth Dean down below. At the bottom the path swings right to a small gate in a wall, and a narrow sunken path (Gib Lane) descends onto a quiet road. *This old road to Haworth is now only a rough track where it crosses the watershed further north.*

Turn right past farm buildings, and just a little further a deeply enclosed path (Lumb Lane), flagged in its lower stages, descends steeply to Crimsworth Dean Beck, turning right at the bottom to Lumb Bridge and Lumb Hole waterfall. *This is a stunning moment, stone-arched packhorse bridge and falls forming a delectable scene. The late Poet Laureate and local man Ted Hughes is recalled here.* Cross the bridge and a path rises away downstream, but as the main path climbs steeply right between walls, pass through an old gateway in front onto a narrower path. *Stoodley Pike is seen far ahead.*

Remaining parallel with the beck, the path contours delightfully through several bracken-filled pastures, eventually encountering a sturdy wall-stile at the end. Passing to the rear of the humble dwelling of Outwood follow its grassy drive to reach a gate into National Trust woodland. Ignore this however in favour of a gap to its left, and a part-flagged path slants down across the field to a stile into the woods. A path runs down to the stone-arched Weet Ing Bridge which is not crossed, continuing instead on the same bank, rising a little then running along towards a gate into a field. One hundred yards before it however, rise half-right on a thinner but clear path slanting up to join the main drive. This is followed left all the way back down to Midgehole, ignoring any branches. Early open views are enjoyed, and beyond an old quarry a firmer access road comes in. Into trees this becomes surfaced at Hollin Hall for the final stage back to the start.

Lumb Hole waterfall, Crimsworth Dean

ABOVE HEPTONSTALL

START Heptonstall   Grid ref. SD 987280

DISTANCE 5 miles (8km)

ORDNANCE SURVEY MAPS
1:50,000
Landranger 103 - Blackburn & Burnley
1:25,000
Explorer OL21 - South Pennines

ACCESS Start from the village centre. Car parks. Served by bus from Hebden Bridge.

> *A splendid amble as a wedge of heather moorland divides two deep wooded valleys, free of any noticeable gradients*

Heptonstall is a fascinating village that merits a leisurely exploration. Steeped in history, it was of greater importance than Hebden Bridge until the arrival of the Industrial Revolution. Its exposed position defended on three sides by precipitous slopes has created a timewarp in which its weather-beaten stone cottages revel. Focal point is the churchyard which separates the imposing parish church of 1854 from the shell of the church of St Thomas a'Becket, partly dating from the 13th century. 'King' David Hartley, notorious coiner, is buried here, as is the poet/writer Sylvia Plath. Alongside is the old grammar school of 1772, now a museum. Seek out also the octagonal Wesleyan chapel (1764), the old dungeon (1824) and the 16th century Cloth Hall. There are two pubs, the Cross Inn and the White Lion, a Post office/shop and a tearoom.

On the main street turn uphill, and beyond the two pubs take the first turn right on Townfield Lane (opposite Weavers Square), continuing past the last of the houses as a walled green lane. *Over to the right are the deep woodlands of Hardcastle Crags, with*

Crimsworth Dean striking away directly ahead. When the way emerges into a field, advance to the next wall corner ahead, then bear left across a couple of fields to join a road. Go briefly left to a stile in the opposite wall, and while a short path goes on towards a stile overlooking the valley of Hebden Water, instead turn left on a thin fieldside path. This immediately commences a superb, largely level course just above and then in the top of Hebden Wood for some time. A fork is reached just after a natural viewing platform: ignore that into the trees, and turn up an enclosed path, leaving it at once by a stile on the right. Across a field the path resumes on the wood top, then soon begins a short descent through the trees. Its level course resumes a short way down, and is maintained for some time until a further descent to run on to the hairpin bend of a wide track. This old route from Gibson Mill now leads steadily uphill. *Just below is the mill, passed on WALK 2 in the valley of Hebden Water.* The path leaves the trees at a gate/stile and rises onto the road alongside a car park at Clough Hole.

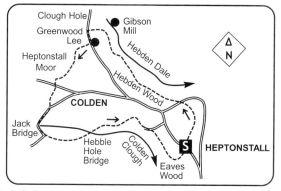

Go left for two minutes to Greenwood Lee on the left. *This is a superb example of a yeoman clothier's house: dating from 1712 it features a splendid great barn of similar age alongside.* Opposite this take a stile on the right into a very slender pasture, rising into a field where a thin trod rises right to a gate/stile halfway up. This puts you onto a corner of Heptonstall Moor, and a thin path rises left with the wall to a cross-paths at the top. Cross and rise left to join another ascending wall, up the moorside to be briefly joined by the Pennine Way by the farmhouse at Mount Pleasant. The path goes on over the brow, where a cairn marks the highest point of the walk at around 1200ft/366m. *This fine tract of heather moorland enjoys big views, especially northwards to a great sweep of high moorland from Gorple Stones around to Midgley Moor.*

Keep straight on towards a final corner of moorland: advance on the main path, and as it drops left to a corner gate, instead take a thin trod slanting right to a corner stile just below. *Ahead are views south over Jack Bridge and Colden to Stoodley Pike.* Entering green pastures head away with an old wall on your left, dropping into a curious, deeply-enclosed little footway. This joins a drive, with a road just below. A few steps to the right take a corner-stile opposite and descend the fieldside, largely with an old paved way underfoot. Just short of the bottom it swings left to a stile onto a road. Turn right with an early footway down through Colden, past the school to Jack Bridge where the New Delight pub awaits.

Just up the road behind it turn left at a hairpin bend along an access road. Ignoring a right branch keep on above a house, and the way becomes a pleasant bridleway on the edge of rapidly forming Colden Clough. A lovely tract of open country develops, and soon a thinner path drops left down the heathery bank to Hebble Hole Bridge. *This ancient footbridge consists of two sets of great stone slabs in a charming location on Colden Water. You are now on an old panniermens' way towards Heptonstall, while the Pennine Way and Calderdale Way also have one of their two meetings here.*

Across the bridge the path slants up to the right, soon reaching a fork. Ignore that rising left in favour of a better-flagged path to the right, running between the fields and the drop to the beck. On entering Foster Wood a stile is met at a kink in the accompanying wall, and here the stone causeway vacates the environs of the beck to cross several fields. *The church tower appears ahead, along with the lower half of densely wooded Colden Clough.* When the flags end the path becomes enclosed before merging with a similar way to rise to a junction with a surfaced access road. Go right, passing above a house to a stile where a further paved section leads to yet another enclosed path at a seat. Turn down it, but keep left at a fork to run a level course to join a narrow access road. Head up this a short way until a path strikes off right. Initially a clamber through the bouldery wood top, keep to the upper path at all times as a grand level walk ensues high above Colden Water, soon opening out above Eaves Wood.

This final stage gives dramatic views from gritstone outcrops down steep heather and bilberry-clad slopes into Colden Clough. Particularly grand is Stoodley Pike, seen from valley floor to the towering monument. The path remains with the left-hand wall until an enclosed path strikes off left. To finish keep straight on between houses to emerge beneath the church. Past here there are a couple of minor branches that lead back onto the main street.

Opposite: Hebble Hole Bridge   *Greenwood Lee*

HEPTONSTALL MOOR

START *Clough Hole   Grid ref. SD 969297*

DISTANCE *6 miles (9^{1}2km)*

ORDNANCE SURVEY MAPS
1:50,000
Landranger 103 - Blackburn & Burnley
1:25,000
Explorer OL21 - South Pennines

ACCESS *Start from the National Trust's Clough Hole car park on the Widdop road a long mile and a half beyond Heptonstall. Summer weekend bus from Hebden Bridge.*

> *A superb mixture of deep woodland and open moorland*

From the car park descend a path outside a wooded clough, crossing it part way down and dropping to a gate into the woods of Hardcastle Crags. The broad way swings down to the right, and very soon a lesser but clear path branches left for a similar slant down through the trees. Ignoring some steep stone steps, the path drops to rejoin the main way which has now doubled back. Bear left to conclude on the valley floor, along to the packhorse bridge at Gibson Mill. *This was founded in 1800 as an early water-powered cotton mill: it ceased to operate in the 1890s, becoming an oddly-sited dance hall and even a roller-skating rink during the mid-20th century. The well-preserved building is an imposing sight in its wooded environs, and features a row of workers' cottages, as well as a cafe, WCs, shop, information, and also exhibitions.*

Resume by returning to your bank of Hebden Water and tracing it upstream. Opposite is the millpond, and just a little further the path climbs stone steps to a higher, very natural looking pond. The path runs along its right bank then resumes beneath cliffs. This is a classic beckside stroll on a largely firm path to a fork beneath stately beeches. Take the right one to remain with the beck, quickly reaching a footbridge. This serves only to avoid a craggy impasse, for just a minute further a second one returns you to your original bank. On again, the path runs to another footbridge. While the main path crosses it, instead take a much thinner one in front to emerge within a few strides on a much broader continuation. This immediately starts to climb from the valley floor, then levels out to run a splendid course, with views through well spaced beeches to the beck. At a hairpin bend ignore the lesser continuation and slant back up to the wood top, where another fine way is joined and followed right. *This is the course of the railway built to bring materials to the Walshaw Dean reservoirs construction site.*

The path runs on past substantial old quarried cliffs that have long been reclaimed by nature, to unexpectedly emerge at the end into some beautiful open country. This is Blake Dean, a superb mix of heather, scrub, bilberry and

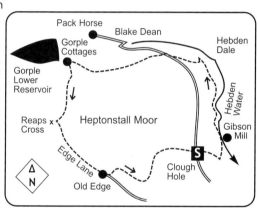

bracken. The path runs on a short way to a path junction. Go left for a steep, stone-stepped climb, passing a well-sited seat before rising to a bridle-gate onto the road at Widdop Gate. Just a few strides to your right turn off along the Gorple Lower Reservoir road, a splendid stride which soon slants up the grassy moor. *The dam of the reservoir appears ahead, with the white-walled Pack Horse Inn appearing to the right.* A superb level promenade leads along the moor in the company of an unseen drain. *The views from this section are magnificent, as you run parallel with Ridge Scout across the deep little divide of Graining Water.*

Just a few steps short of isolated Gorple Cottages the Pennine Way is met. Follow it on the broad track up to the left, bridging the drain to rise up the moor. *Gorple Lower Reservoir now appears back to your right. Reaching a gate, lean on it to look back over a panoramic moorscape to the north.* Through the intervening gate the Pennine Way goes off left, but you remain on the track over the brow of Heptonstall Moor. Whilst climbing, a quarry site is passed on the right where stone was won for reservoir construction. Nearing the brow you will see the conspicuous Reaps Cross on the moor to the right, and just five minutes away it merits a detour. Possibly dating from medieval times, it stands in its own base astride an old moorland packway. Its upper section has been restored this century to stand a proud ten-foot tall. A thin trod cuts back to rejoin the track, which quickly runs down to a gate off the moor. *Ahead is the Colden Valley backed by a sweeping Calderdale skyline.*

The unsurfaced access road of Edge Lane heads away, and remains underfoot for almost a mile. Becoming surfaced at New Edge on your left, advance just a short way further to the houses at Old Edge on your right. Immediately after them take a gate on the left and ascend a wallside, the upper section enclosed by old walls to reach a wall-stile onto Heptonstall Moor. An inviting little path turns right, running a grand course through the heather. Quickly approaching a wall corner at recolonised quarries, a left branch to the outer corner sees you resume along the moor edge. At the end comes a bigger corner: once again go left on a clearer wallside path to another outer corner. This time go straight ahead, a good little path slanting to the left down through dense heather, bearing further left to approach a curving wall corner.

Just short of the wall the broader Pennine Way is met again. Cross straight over to a stile in the wall below, and a neat little path crosses the pasture to the barn at Clough Head. Behind it a gap-stile in the wall puts you onto a final corner of moorland. Drop right to the right-hand stile by a gate, and an old sunken way drops down a pasture. *Nice views look down Hardcastle Crags backed by Midgley Moor.* At the bottom is a cross-paths alongside Clough House: through the gate ahead bear left to another gate beneath the house. A grassy track runs on to join the drive, which leads back down onto the road at the start.

START Widdop   Grid ref. SD 946323

DISTANCE 6^{1}2 miles (10^{1}2km)

ORDNANCE SURVEY MAPS
1:50,000
Landranger 103 - Blackburn & Burnley
1:25,000
Explorer OL21 - South Pennines

ACCESS Start from the roadside parking area near Clough Foot, half a mile west of the Pack Horse inn on the Heptonstall-Colne road. Summer weekend bus from Hebden Bridge. •ACCESS NOTE: Open Access, see page 8. The path from Walshaw to Walshaw Dean is a permissive path on Savile Estate land, and may be closed on certain days in the grouse shooting season and at times of high fire risk. An alternative is mentioned at the relevant point.

Good paths traverse open country above Hardcastle Crags, from rock-strewn and part-wooded valley to bare heather moorland

From the lay-by follow the road south-east towards the well-named pub. However, beyond a lone house take a bridle-gate on the right giving access to a short-lived green way. At the end go left with a crumbling wall along the edge of the deep little clough. The path soon reaches a fork. The right branch descends to a charming watersmeet in the narrow valley of Graining Water: it is well seen from above. Your route keeps straight on by the wall: skirting the pronounced drop it becomes clearer when the old wall departs and the gritstone outcrops of Ridge Scout appear. Beyond the first rocks the path starts a gentle descent, slanting into denser bracken after a second, larger group, then running on beneath the largest group of outcrops to a stile onto a hairpin bend of the road.

The building in front is on the site of a Baptist Chapel of 1802: the burial ground survives. Turn downhill to a drive on the left before the bridge, quickly leaving it as a stile sends a stepped path down to a footbridge on Alcomden Water in Blake Dean. *This beauty spot features a colourful watersmeet with grassy banks and green islands beneath steep slopes.* Take the main path climbing away, and when a broad green path comes along from an old railway cutting, turn right on it. *Shortly, down below, five footings can clearly be seen: these supported a 700ft/215m long trestle viaduct which carried a railway 100ft/30m above the beck, constructed in 1901 to transport materials to Walshaw Dean reservoir site.* On reaching a stile a slimmer path runs on through the bracken, then through and above woodland to the isolated house at Over Wood. A cart track takes over to head into the deeper woods at the head of Hebden Dale.

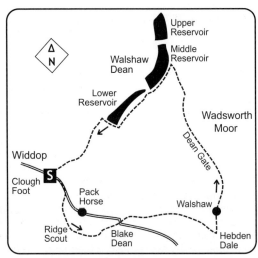

After about ten minutes, as you reach the valley floor, a bridge is reached at a sidestream: without advancing to the path junction just across it, turn left up a narrow path immediately before the stream. It rises through an old gateway on the right and climbs steeply above the stream, remaining close to it as other branches go left. At the wood top go left a few strides to a small gate into a field, then rise towards Walshaw shooting lodge. *With its enviable view down-dale, it dates from the 1860s, part of a very attractive and ancient farming hamlet.* Just to the right of the lodge a tiny enclosure is entered by a gate and left by a corner stile a little higher, putting you into the yard. The enclosed track rising directly from the top end is your route, assuming there are no signs to the contrary. If there should be, then turn left on the broad bridleway track between the buildings, and it runs unerringly on to rejoin the main route near the walk's conclusion.

On heading up the track, leave it as soon as it turns sharp left to New Cote Farm, immediately after another drive has gone right. A little path branches off up a small tract of open ground. Rejoining a track at a gate just above, this ascends the wallside to become enclosed at the top. It rises pleasantly to emerge onto the open moor. Ignoring the track ascend straight up a narrow path to quickly meet the track again at a fork. Take the left branch straight ahead, over a shoulder of Wadsworth Moor. *Known as Dean Gate, this old path is now a Landrover track, though it remains very pleasant underfoot.* It attains the walk's summit at some 1380ft/420m, with sweeping views of heather-clad moors. *Gorple Upper and Widdop reservoirs are seen over to the left, with Black Hameldon and Boulsworth Hill on the high western skyline.* The descent towards Walshaw Dean sees its reservoirs soon appear. Just beneath a stone shooting box is a fork. The left branch is slightly shorter, but the better route goes straight on down to a gate/stile in a wall. Just beyond this it bridges a drain alongside Walshaw Dean Middle Reservoir. Here double back left on the Pennine Way which runs a good course between drain and reservoir.

The trio of reservoirs occupying the floor of Walshaw Dean was begun in 1900 and the reservoirs officially opened in 1907, but leakage problems meant the job was only fully completed in 1915. With three reservoirs under construction the workforce peaked at more than 500 men, most accommodated at a lively shanty town nearby. At the end you bridge the drain to rejoin a track, but don't follow it across the dam to the former keeper's house. Instead go straight ahead on the Pennine Way, a firm path running a generally level course beneath a sturdy wall above the full length of the lower reservoir. Bridging the outflow at the end, cross the grassy embankment and up onto the surfaced reservoir road. Turning left this leads back to the start, avoiding a pair of left forks and passing a plantation. Dropping to a bend just before the road, a bridle-gate on the left cuts out a small corner to gain the lay-by.

GORPLE MOORS

START Widdop   Grid ref. SD 946323

DISTANCE 5 miles (8km)

ORDNANCE SURVEY MAPS
1:50,000
Landranger 103 - Blackburn & Burnley
1:25,000
Explorer OL21 - South Pennines

ACCESS Start from the roadside parking area at Clough Foot, half a mile west of the Pack Horse Inn, where the Gorple reservoir road leaves the Heptonstall-Colne road. Summer weekend bus from Hebden Bridge. •ACCESS NOTE: Open Access, see page 8. Some water company permissive paths, all within Open Access land.

A trio of moorland waters linked by pleasant paths and tracks

From the lay-by take the gate across the road and head away along a reservoir road rising to the dam of Gorple Lower Reservoir. Don't cross, take the right branch to continue alongside the water and its feeder Reaps Water. Remain on this until rising to the dam of the second sheet of water, Gorple Upper Reservoir. *En route you encounter several stands of trees, patches of heather, and a wooden shooters' cabin with the impressive Dicken Rocks ranged up behind it. The two Gorple Reservoirs were completed in 1934.* Again don't cross the dam, instead cross the small drain just before it on the right and take a thin path climbing directly up the slope of Shuttleworth Moor. Initially steep, it soon eases to rise through various outcrops, some of these rock formations being impressively substantial. The path continues up this broad tongue to join a wide track, the Gorple Gate. *At around 1410ft/430m this highest point of the walk is astride an old way over the moors to*

Worsthorne in Lancashire, and would have been at its busiest in packhorse days. Big views look west to the moors south of Burnley, while eastwards the Pack Horse Inn looks diminutive amid a Calderdale landscape looking towards Stoodley Pike.

Turn right along the track, which at once begins a gentle descent. Widdop Reservoir soon appears ahead, backed by a high craggy edge. After dropping steeply left to a hairpin bend, branch left on a contrastingly narrow path. With the remains of a wall just below, this drops gradually beneath steep slopes towards the head of the reservoir. Just beyond it the wall finally drops away and the path forks. Drop right to a footbridge, a few strides beyond which a broad green track is joined. Go right, soon reaching a wall where you pass between it and a drain for a few steps before crossing the drain by a footbridge. Head left on a splendid little grassy path's infallible course between drain and reservoir.

Widdop Reservoir was completed in 1878 to supply the thirsts of Halifax townsfolk more than 50 years before the walk's two other reservoirs: it almost equals their joint capacities. Materials were brought to the site by means of a 5¼-mile long horse-drawn tramway from further

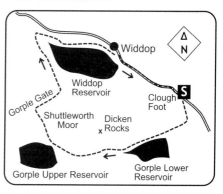

down the valley. Some bold gritstone crags flank the reservoir to the north. When the trees disappear a grassy track comes in, still tracing the shore until beyond a couple of houses at Widdop Lodge it re-crosses the drain and heads up to the road. Go right on this largely unfenced moor road, past Clough Foot to the start. *The moorland Colne-Heptonstall road was an important trans-Pennine packhorse route three centuries ago, lime and cloth being major goods. Shortly after leaving the dam, look back over your right shoulder to see a giant 'rocking' stone perched on one of the moor edge buttresses at Cludders Slack.*

BRIDE STONES

START *Lydgate   Grid ref. SD 923255*

DISTANCE *5^{3}4 miles (9km)*

ORDNANCE SURVEY MAPS
1:50,000
Landranger 103 - Blackburn & Burnley
1:25,000
Explorer OL21 - South Pennines

ACCESS *Lydgate is 1^{1}4 miles north of Todmorden on the Burnley road (A646). Street parking. Served by Todmorden-Burnley bus.*

> *A fascinating perambulation around the rock formations and outstanding causeyed packways high above Todmorden*

Leave the main road by Church Road next to the Post office/shop, and at the end bear right on a private-looking drive, Owlers Walk. An enclosed path passes to the right of the last house and on beneath a rail embankment to emerge at an immense railway arch. Pass underneath it on a drive but almost at once take a small gate on the right to ascend an old flight of stone steps to a small gate at the top. *Stannally House is seen over to the left.*

Resume up the fieldside above, and when the fence goes left, go straight up a distinct hollow, and continue steeply up to reach isolated Rake Farm. Go right of the house to a path junction on the driveway, then pass behind the rear house to a gate. From it a super old way rises away above the garden and up to an intriguing corner stile in colourful surroundings. *The knoll of Wirlaw rises impressively back over the house.* Don't use the stile but remain on the path slanting right up to a small gate into a walled way. This climbs then runs left to another bend in front of the open country of Stannally Stones.

Advance straight on the little wallside path along its base to meet a driveway: follow this very briefly to the wall corner ahead. *Prominent further ahead are Orchan Rocks: when you reach these, the walk is almost over!* As the track turns left down between walls, leave it in favour of a delightful little footpath climbing straight up through heather and bracken to join a walled green lane at the top corner. This splendid track is the old packhorse route of Stony Lane, with which you are to become well acquainted. *The views are very typical Calderdale: windfarm, populated valley floor, moors, farms, rocks, and the Cliviger and Walsden gorges.*

Mount Cross

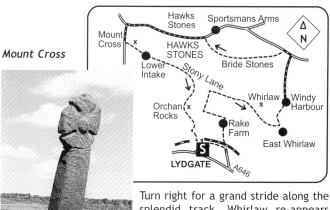

Turn right for a grand stride along the splendid track. Whirlaw re-appears directly ahead, and an early briefly flagged section features before soon emerging to cross a reedy pasture on flags to a gate onto Whirlaw Common. Two flagged paths head away: take the one bearing right, a superb way curving beneath Whirlaw Stones, remaining flagged until becoming enclosed again. *Just prior to this Stoodley Pike appears across the valley. Whirlaw Stones form a well-defined edge high above your causeway, gritstone boulders interlaced with patches of heather.* A couple of minutes further, above East Whirlaw Farm, double back left up a wallside track. This swings right above the wall and climbs further, closing in on the wall again to rise to a gate/stile at the top right-hand corner.

33

The terminus of Windy Harbour Lane is joined at a crossroads with green tracks. *Alongside is an enterprisingly carved stone gatepost.* After an initially very steep pull past Windy Harbour Farm it levels out at a mast to run on to meet Eastwood Road. *Ahead is a vast sweep of moorland.* Go left only as far as the end of the left-hand wall, where a stile sends a green path across Bride Stones Moor to the prominent outcrops of the same name. *The Great Bride Stones are the most extensive group of rocks on the walk, and the first of these include a particularly remarkable detached rock resembling its North York Moors' namesakes (see page 1).* The Ordnance Survey column at 1437ft/438m marks the highest point of the walk. Advance on either the base or the crest of the main rocks. *You may well see rock climbers enjoying their sport here.* Below you a distinctive fang of rock overlooks a fence-stile, but ignore this and forge on a higher, largely level course to a further cluster in line with the Coal Clough windfarm immediately above Bride Stones Farm.

Bear right above the later rocks, and a grassy track comes in on the right to lead to a gate/stile onto an access road beyond the last rocks. Turn right the short way onto Kebs Road. *The Sportsmans Arms is just two minutes along to the right, if needed.* The route goes left along the road for a good level three-quarters of a mile through the scattered settlement of Hawks Stones. *Known as the Long Causeway, this ancient route between Burnley and Halifax affords extensive views to high moorland skylines. High above are the Hawks Stones, a line of outcrops resembling bears on hind legs. A little before a bend is a roadside stone inscribed 'Hawk Stones 1902': the turbines of Coal Clough windfarm are also very close now. Precisely as you reach a junction at the bend, the familiar whaleback of Pendle Hill is seen far ahead.* Turn left down Mount Lane just as far as a walled track opposite a farm on the right. *This spot is a junction of old packhorse routes, as Mount Lane meets the rough Stony Lane.* First encountered during the approach to Whirlaw, Stony Lane's mostly level course is now followed in that direction (left), initially as a farm access road.

Almost immediately a glance over the upper wall reveals Mount Cross. *Standing forlornly amidst munching sheep, this is thought to date back to monastic times, as a waymarker on a route serving Whalley Abbey in the Ribble Valley.* Just beyond, at Lower

Intake, the way has a brief narrow section as it passes left of the farm, then resumes more broadly. A short flagged section features as you drop down to bridge Redmires Water beneath a scattered plantation. On the brow comes a level section, just beyond which a gateway on the right sends a wallside track down towards flat-topped Orchan Rocks. Part way down you can opt for a fence-stile on the right, a few strides beyond which a thin path drops parallel, meeting a sunken, level path curving round to the top of the rocks, a splendid location. Drop down either side and go left to rejoin the track at a stile. At the bottom corner it goes through a gateway: from it drop left to meet another track in another corner.

Through a gate/stile the track becomes enclosed, and at once absorbs a farm drive which leads all the way down, largely through the trees of Kitson Wood, to the valley bottom. *During this section there is a good view of the rail viaduct through the trees, while the railway itself later passes through a tunnel directly beneath you.* As civilisation is embraced turn left after the first house on a cart track to a steep access road down onto the side street on which the walk began.

The causey across Whirlaw

9

ROBINWOOD

START Todmorden   Grid ref. SD 936241

DISTANCE 6 miles ($9^1$2km)

ORDNANCE SURVEY MAPS
1:50,000
Landranger 103 - Blackburn & Burnley
1:25,000
Explorer OL21 - South Pennines

ACCESS Start from the town centre. Car parks. Served by bus and train from Halifax and Rochdale, and by bus from Burnley.

An absorbing exploration of the western dale side north of Todmorden, featuring woodland, moorland and valley flanks

Todmorden is a smashing little town with some outstanding buildings. Dobroyd Castle was built in the 1860s for the influential Fielden family, mill owners and local benefactors. The Town Hall was designed by their architect John Gibson in 1875, and features marble figures on a pediment above tall columns. The Old Hall was built in 1603 by the Ratcliffe family, who long preceded the Fieldens in Todmorden circles: it has a fantastic intricate frontage of gables and mullioned and transomed windows. St Mary's parish church is central but tucked away, while the more outgoing Unitarian Church of 1869 boasts a tall spire. Unlike its counterparts which thrived on the woollen industry, Todmorden and its mills were geared to the Lancashire cotton industry; indeed until little over a century ago Todmorden was literally on the border. Of the three roads heading out, two still aim for the red rose towns of Rochdale and Burnley, both more accessible than Todmorden's Yorkshire masters: a hint of divided loyalties remains hereabouts!

From the roundabout head south on the Rochdale road, and quickly turn up Rise Lane on the right. *At once on the left is the Old Hall.* Continue up past the station and under the rail bridge. The road climbs steeply away, but leave it almost at once by the very steep Ridge Steps climbing onto Well Lane. Virtually opposite, a broad, surfaced pathway heads off. *Below, you have a good view over the town viaduct backed by Stoodley Pike.* The level path curves steadily into trees. Ignoring any lesser branches, this same paths runs all the way on to a fork above an open area of Centre Vale Park: here take the unsurfaced left branch which slants very gently up to quickly emerge onto a narrow road, Ewood Lane.

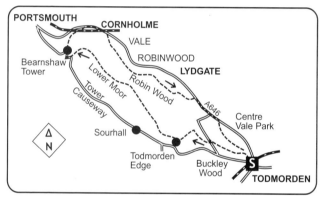

Turn briefly left up the road then take a path doubling back right to begin a long, steady pull through delectable beechwood. At the top is an airy level section before being deposited into a field. *The view back over the valley sees the prominent knoll of Whirlaw now topped by higher ground, as well as the Bride Stones, Hawks Stones and the Long Causeway. Looking back are Stoodley Pike, Walsden Moor and Blackstone Edge.* Go left up the wallside, becoming enclosed at the end to rise pleasantly as a grassy way to a rough access road at Todmorden Edge. *Todmorden Edge Farm was a Friends' Meeting House, with a Quaker graveyard alongside.* Go right a short way, and take the first of two adjacent gates on the left opposite the last building. Head away, rising slightly along the wallside, a part-enclosed section being sunken and a little moist.

Emerging, don't go on to the far end, but take a gate on the right to resume on the wall's other side, with a fence taking over at an intervening stile. *Over to the right is a rich mix of country, with moorland patches such as Whirlaw and Stannally Stones in amongst wall-patterned fields: Coal Clough windfarm is ahead.* From a gate at the end bear gently left up the field to one opposite. Through sheep pens a gate/stile admits onto a corner of Lower Moor.

Advance the few yards up onto a drive, and bear right on it past a reedy pool at an old quarry. Ignore an immediate branch down to a house, and keep straight on to the next house (West End). Directly above it, leave the track for a thin path slanting up onto the moor. It quickly levels out to meet a cross-paths: keep right to contour along not far above the track, passing above another renovated farmhouse at New Towneley and still contouring to approach the final one. During this a broader path slants up from the right to merge, and rises slightly to run on until above the last house where the access road finally ends. Here your path also fragments at a crossroads with a sunken way coming in from the left.

Keep to the upper path which contours on still further, above an old enclosure then thinly on above reeds bound for the house at Height Top ahead. This super little path runs on and rises slightly to join the drive. Follow it right down to the entrance, which is avoided by going left on a little path to join a wallside grass track to the left. Resume along this, soon becoming a little rougher as it drops away from the wall, with Portsmouth in the valley floor ahead and a large plantation to your left. The track drops down to a sharp bend of a moorland road, Tower Causeway. Turn right down this off the moor, briefly down to another such bend at Bearnshaw Tower. Go right here on a little path between buildings to emerge into a sloping pasture. An old green way crosses to a gate/stile opposite, from where a super fenceside path runs down a little ridge overlooking a curious dry hollow. At the bottom it becomes an enclosed green way, curving right beneath heather banks and above civilization. Merging into a rough access road it goes right to houses at Frostholme, where as Stubley Lane it drops under a rail arch to emerge onto the main road in Cornholme.

Cross and follow the footway right, passing under the railway again in the process. *Cornholme has the Waggon & Horses pub, a shop and Post office.* Immediately before the church of St Michael

& All Angels turn right up a short, rough street: at the end a path rises left to a stile at the foot of a colourful bank, then slants splendidly left across it. *Big views look back over the village and the uppermost dale, and the windfarm quickly returns.* Towards the top you reach a well-defined promontory (where Stoodley Pike appears ahead), concluding with a steep little pull, on through an old wall and on to the head of a tiny stream. This is the high point of the return path: across it the way resumes, slanting left beneath an old wall as a mercurial green way.

This super path winds around further with the wall to reveal the view 'down-dale'. It slants superbly down under the craggy flanks of Barewise Wood, faithfully down to the valley floor. *The Staff of Life pub at Robinwood is seen on the roadside below.* The path emerges onto a drive at a bridge alongside the road. Don't cross, but turn right on an access road. At the house gates, don't enter the driveway but take a gate/stile on the right, and a rough path rises away beneath scattered Robin Wood. This improves above a circular pond and runs on beneath a wall, rising slightly to a stile at the end. *Look back to see an archetypal Calderdale landscape shared by the likes of Orchan Rocks and a mighty railway viaduct.* Two faint old grassy paths head away: take the left one rising slightly, then contouring on through a part-wooded hollow before rising briefly to join a broader green path. Turn down this to a stile into the woods, and a fine path slants down to the rear of Scaitcliff Hall, currently a hotel, then going left down onto the main road at Gate Bottom.

Go right for a couple of minutes, past a school and Ewood Lane to reach Central Vale Park. *Bought from the Fielden family in 1910, it features a fine statue of John Fielden, MP for Oldham: he was instrumental in the passing of the 10 Hour Act in 1847, which meant women and children were saved from working more than 10 hours per day!* You can find your own way from here, emerging at the end to continue the final few minutes back into the centre of town. Best option is to aim for the church tower, leaving the right-hand far corner of the park behind a playground, rising briefly to a level path that goes left into trees behind the cricket club to emerge on a road-end above the sombre Christ Church of 1834. Either keep straight on to rejoin the outward route on Well Lane, or turn down steps past the church onto the main road.

FREEHOLDS TOP

START Gauxholme   Grid ref. SD 929231

DISTANCE 6^14 miles (10km)

ORDNANCE SURVEY MAPS
1:50,000
Landranger 103 - Blackburn & Burnley
1:25,000
Explorer OL21 - South Pennines

ACCESS Start from the rail viaduct at the junction of the A681 Bacup road, a short mile south of Todmorden town centre. Parking on the Bacup road. Served by Todmorden-Rochdale bus.

A reasonably strenuous ramble in Upper Calder country, with broad uplands atop steep gradients from the industrial valley

At Gauxholme a long, low railway viaduct straddles the main junction, with the Masons Arms and a craft brewery sheltering beneath. The Woodpecker Inn is just along the road towards Todmorden. From the main road pass under the viaduct, pass the pub and head away over the canal bridge, then turn left on short-lived Naze Road. Take a gate on the left alongside modern housing, and a broad green track heads away. Doubling back almost at once, a steep climb of The Naze ensues, featuring a cleverly engineered and thoroughly enjoyable zigzag. *This next mile traces an old pack-horse route from Todmorden towards Rochdale. The map-like view of the cramped industrial valley floor with its railway, road, canal and mills, is in stark contrast with the hillside's crumbling walls and reedy pastures.*

As the gradient eases the climb continues between old walls to a brief enclosed section emptying onto the open moor. Go forward to join a wide track, and briefly left on it. As it bears left at a wall corner take the lesser fork straight ahead, tracing a stone causey gently rising arrow-like across the otherwise soggy moorland of Inchfield Pasture. At a beck crossing the path deteriorates a little, but forges straight on to join the broad, unsurfaced Foul Clough Road by Thorns Greece Farm. Turn right, sweeping around above the intake wall to its demise at a gate above the last house. *Down to the left is the drained Ramsden Clough Reservoir of 1888.*

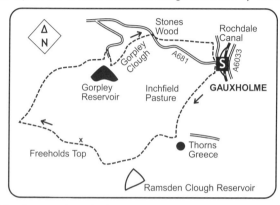

The improved track rises past a ruin to a fork: take the right one to maintain the climb by a walled enclosure, then swinging away to rise by a small stream. With the sombre ruin of Coolam over to the left the track rises to a fence junction: from the gate ahead it enters the moor. Take the firmer track rising with a fence then rising right above it to the grassed-over spoil and ruinous buildings of an old mine. Here take a narrow path rising behind, past a larger spoil heap. This short, steep climb on easy grass pulls right to impressively gain the Ordnance Survey column on Freeholds Top. *With a novel summit pool, at 1489ft/454m this is one of the highest points in Calderdale, and an extensive view-point. Its panorama is very much an upland one: high landmarks occupy the Pennine watershed to north and south in the shape of Black Hameldon and Blackstone Edge respectively, while to the east is Stoodley Pike, and westwards the industry-ravaged moors of Rossendale. A welcome intrusion through the Cliviger Gorge is the unmistakable outline of Pendle Hill.*

From the gate alongside go left with the fence on a thin trod to a junction, there turning right with fence and old wall along the broad ridge top. *The county boundary with Lancashire occupies this section, which is likely to be moist in parts.* As the fence parts company keep straight on, a rather exceptional wall soon taking its place. When a normal wall resumes, a reedy pool will be seen just over it. Just beyond it a ladder-stile is reached: don't use it, but instead depart the ridge on a thin path descending right directly away across surprisingly dry grass (ignore a thinner left branch) to quickly join an old mine road at some former workings.

Crossing straight over, the thin trod continues down otherwise rough terrain towards the head of the deep clough of Range Hoyle. A path encircling it swings along to the left above a collapsed wall. Follow this round and then away as it skirts a pronounced drop to Gorpley Reservoir (1904). After an intervening fence-stile a fence takes over and a thinner trod continues gently down until a grass track materialises. *On nearing the reservoir note a deep cleft on its opposite bank with a tiny finger of water reaching in: one might forget its artificial nature.* The track soon drops down to a small house, Keepers Lodge. Go left along the drive and down to meet a road. Turn right to descend to the treatment plant below the dam.

From a small gate on the left towards the bottom, descend a part-stepped path into Gorpley Clough. This is a charming wooded dell whose tinkling stream enjoys two enchanting moments, the lower pair of cascades being especially delectable. This same path leads unerringly down, crossing and re-crossing the beck on two occasions to finally emerge onto the Bacup road. Turn briefly right on the footway past an old mill, then escape at a gap on the left beyond a house. A path rises through Stones Wood, leaving by a kissing-gate after a small clough. The path crosses two fields to a junction of old green ways: rise left between walls, and through the gate/stile at the top turn right to cross a field bottom. From a stile at the end go on past a stable block at Watty Farm, and just past the house is a wall-stile onto a tiny green way. A few strides to the left this meets a steep path dramatically perched above the valley. *The first heather of the walk is in evidence at this late stage, but it is the stunning bird's-eye view that holds attention.* Turn down the quickly broadening path to return to Gauxholme, emerging onto Pexwood Road just short of the main road.

11

WALSDEN MOOR

START Warland   Grid ref. SD 944200

DISTANCE 6^{1}4 miles (10km)

ORDNANCE SURVEY MAPS
1:50,000
Landranger 103 - Blackburn & Burnley
1:25,000
Explorer OL21 - South Pennines

ACCESS Start from the Bird i'th' Hand pub on the main road. Roadside parking outside of double yellow lines: lay-by a little to the north. Served by Todmorden-Rochdale bus.

> Sustained interest from towpath to moor top: easy to follow paths include a historic packhorse route

From the pub cross the road and take the lane (Warland Gate End) heading away to cross the Rochdale Canal alongside Warland Middle Lock. *The bridge marks the county boundary.* Keep on the lane between two houses as it starts a long climb to the moor. *At a sharp bend the whitewashed cottages on the left feature a 1655 datestone.* At a brief levelling out take the right arm at a fork, bridging a stream to a gate to rise again before swinging right to reach Calflee House. Follow the track up to its left, rising to a restored house just above. From a gate/stile above its rear corner a path slants up the grassy moor to a gateway above, to then rise in harmony with the adjacent beck past some boulders.

The going quickly eases out and the grassy retaining wall of Warland Reservoir is equally quickly revealed ahead. The path broadens, and on nearing the embankment, it rises gently right as a broad track to gain the southern corner of the reservoir. *Far to the north Coal Clough windfarm spreads itself across the noble breast of mighty Pendle Hill.* Cross straight over the reservoir road and over a connecting footbridge onto a thin path along the grassy embankment of neighbouring Light Hazzles Reservoir. *Warland and Light Hazzles reservoirs were built to supply water to the canal, completed in 1804. Within forty years railways had ensured its early demise, and by 1922 commercial traffic had virtually ceased: the following year the reservoirs were sold to local authorities.*

At the far end of the reedy reservoir head, the path advances a few fainter steps then turns a few paces left to a simple foot-bridge over a small clough. The thin but clear path immediately improves as it goes right to then quickly swing left on the distinct embankment of a long-defunct drain. It runs a dead-level course into increasing heather, with only one brief moist section. Nearing Warland Reservoir again you pass just below extensive boulder-slopes at Stony Edge. *Here you find heather and gritstone in harmony, a good place for a break.* The reservoir track is regained upon striding a concrete drain at the most northerly point of the reservoir.

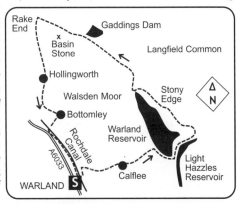

Follow the hard track right just as far as a sharp bend. *Stoodley Pike appears almost at once, some way ahead along the moorland edge of Langfield Common.* Here strike left across the moor on a firmly flagged path in the direction of Gaddings Dam. *Wind turbines now surround you, at a distance, with Ovenden Moor to the right, Coal Clough straight ahead, and Scout Moor (the UK's largest onshore site, completed in 2008) due left.* The flags lead unfailingly very gently down until you leave peaty, moist moor for flat, dry grassy moor, and a grand path runs on to traverse the left-hand embankment. *Note the embankment of its former twin over to the right.* Below a grandiose flight of steps the broader path continues down the moor, quickly passing the very distinctive Basin Stone and trending right down to a crossroads with a part-paved way, marked by a cairn just short of Rake End. *From here towards Bottomley you follow the well-preserved causeway of Salter Rake, part of a packhorse route used for bringing salt across the Pennines from Cheshire: it has a bird's-eye view of Walsden and across the valley to Ramsden Clough.* Turn left on the path sloping down across the moor, a grand stride acquiring a continuous causeyed surface before entering walled confines at North Hollingworth. Advance along the first drive a short way, and at the junction, with a splendid white-walled old house in front, go left on the drive to Hollingworth Gate.

From a gate beneath the house ignore the wide track up the field, and instead trace the causeway along the field bottom to the end. *This marks an excellent viewpoint, with the canal leading the eye through the Walsden Gorge, and the buttress of Reddyshore Scout opposite.* The causey descends delightfully to the back of the house at Dean Royd, but without entering rises left again to cross to a small bridge over a tiny beck. Across it rise into the hamlet of Bottomley. *This was the site of an early Friends' Meeting House.* Turn briefly right then leave the access road by a gate on the right. An enclosed, cobbled way descends to the canal at Bottomley Lock. *Hidden in a field here is the northern entrance to Summit railway tunnel, scene of a dramatic train fire in 1984.* Go left along the towpath to return to Warland, passing Warland Lower Lock and a reedy pond before finishing along Warland Gate End.

The Basin Stone, Walsden Moor

12

REDDYSHORE SCOUT

START *Walsden   Grid ref. SD 934219*

DISTANCE *6 miles (9½km)*

ORDNANCE SURVEY MAPS
1:50,000
Landranger 103 - Blackburn & Burnley
Landranger 109 - Manchester
1:25,000
Explorer OL21 - South Pennines

ACCESS *Start from the village centre by Post office and church, street parking. Served by Todmorden-Rochdale bus and train.*

Superb walking on green tracks through the impressive surrounds of the Walsden Gorge: quite a history trail too

Walsden is Todmorden's sizeable southerly offshoot, occupying the narrow valley floor of the little seen Walsden Water for some length. Like Todmorden it was part of Lancashire until the late 19th century, and its industrial past focused more on cotton. Today Walsden is best known for its extensive garden centre, with a café. Focal point is where tall-spired St Peter's church and the Post office/shop stand. Close by are a Methodist church (Free Church) of 1861, a chippy, and some intriguing 'tilted' houses. South of the village the railway burrows through the infamous Summit Tunnel, opened in 1840 and the scene of a dramatic train fire in 1984. The tops of its innumerable cylindrical air shafts are seen on the walk.

From the Post office head south, away from Todmorden on the roadside footway: parallel Square Road gives a break from the main road. The main road then bridges the railway and passes the garden centre to reach Bottoms. Alongside the Border Rose pub turn right on Ramsden Wood Road. This soon leaves the village to run past a densely wooded bank and stream to Ramsden Wood, where housing has replaced two mills demolished early in the 21st century. Just past the first houses the road climbs away: keep left on an old lane as the modern road bears right to more housing. Rising away, soon take a signed path on the left, up a few steps and on through trees. Quickly reaching a fence-stile into more open surrounds, a broad, level old way is joined at a cross-paths. Bear left on this, above the wood top and on into a scene of old workings. After the trees end a cairn sends a much thinner path right just as a fence comes up on the left. The thin path runs on beneath steep scree slopes, over a knoll and on to the end of the site, where it slants more distinctly up past a pylon onto open grassy moor above the clough head.

Merging with another thin path keep on with a wall on your right, and as this ends a fence leads on to reach a ladder-stile in the wall at the end. Surrounded now by higher, very solemn moorland, rise left onto the grassy embankment of the hitherto unseen Cranberry Dam. Either go left to trace its embank-

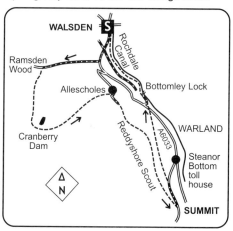

ments, or right to the reservoir head, across knolly terrain just above it, past an old wall end and down to a track dropping through consecutive gates/stiles in fences. Crossing a tiny stream the track rises away to a scant ruin at White Slack, with a delightful little garden. *En route note the deep ravine to your left.* From here the improved level track heads away, initially with the wall, then straight on past a massive standing stone to a gate/stile in a fence enclosing new trees. Remain on this track which soon swings right with a wall down onto an access road opposite Lower Allescholes Farm. Turn right, rising gently past another farm to level out and run along to a sudden demise beneath Moor Hey Farm. Alongside a small wood the old road runs to a gate onto reedy rough pasture.

A superb level track now heads away, quickly passing the Allescholes milestone. *Impressively perched on the hilltop only a couple of steps off the path, it is nevertheless easily missed as you stride on. An outstanding specimen, it bears the distances to Halifax, Todmorden, Rochdale and Burnley. Your outward route traces this centuries-old packhorse route, Reddyshore Scout Gate, high above the Summit Tunnel. Excellent views over Walsden Gorge feature the Rochdale Canal backed by the landmark of Blackstone Edge.* The mercurial green track suddenly finds itself above a craggy drop, with an air shaft by your return route below, and the Bird i'th' Hand pub at Warland seen in true bird's-eye fashion on the valley floor. A gate between two pylons sees the way become enclosed, though in part running even more dramatically atop Reddyshore Scout. *Steep crags add a dramatic foreground to the view: immediately over the canal note the labyrinthine zigzags of old quarrymens' tracks scaling the steep slopes opposite.* The track continues unfailingly, merging into a farm drive to eventually drop between air shafts onto a road.

The canal at Warland from Reddyshore Scout

Turn left down the road as far as an air shaft by Owler Clough. *An old boundary stone stands by the wall on the right.* Here take a gently rising green path on the left back towards Reddyshore Scout. This one however is to run beneath the cliffs, parallel with your outward leg. *Briefly glimpsed on the road below is hexagonal Steanor Bottom Toll House astride a former turnpike junction: its list of charges is admirably preserved.* Rising to a gate beneath a steep crag, the path eases out to run beneath further crags. After a stile below a pylon it crosses to an air shaft to begin a steady descent through bracken to another shaft, just past which it meets a clearer path descending from the Allescholes milestone. This drops pleasantly down the last section and on past a final air shaft to join a drive: cross straight over and down an overgrown cobbled snicket to another drive joining the main road alongside a terrace.

Cross with care and go briefly left to steps onto Bottomley Road. *To the left is the northern entrance to Summit rail tunnel, scene of a dramatic fire in 1984.* Advance past Hilldyke Cottages to the Rochdale Canal at Bottomley Lock. *Completed in 1804, it runs 33 miles between Manchester and the Calder & Hebble Navigation at Sowerby Bridge. Sadly its heyday was a brief one, and the demise began in 1841 when the Lancashire & Yorkshire Railway arrived. Thus the canals, which themselves had replaced packhorses, were quickly ousted by the vastly more efficient rail service.* Go left on the towpath, a splendid stride passing a number of locks descending into Walsden. The temptation of direct access to the Cross Keys comes just a minute from the end, where at Travis Mill Lock you join a road near the church. Turn left on St Peter's Gate to finish.

Allescholes milestone   *Canal milestone*   *Boundary stone*

13

STOODLEY PIKE

START Lumbutts   Grid ref. SD 956234

DISTANCE 7 miles (11km)

ORDNANCE SURVEY MAPS
1:50,000
Landranger 103 - Blackburn & Burnley
1:25,000
Explorer OL21 - South Pennines

ACCESS Start from the village centre. The dead-end road to the Top Brink inn is for patrons, though there are odd corners just up the hill. An alternative start is roadside parking at the Shepherd's Rest, a short mile into the walk. Served by bus from Todmorden.

An exhilarating, easy high-level march on the Lumbutts and Mankinholes skyline to a celebrated Calderdale landmark

Lumbutts is an attractive settlement nestling in a hollow below Mankinholes. It is entirely dominated by a former water wheel tower: this immense structure once contained three vertically arranged wheels, each fed from above as well as independently. It served a cotton mill that once stood here. Immediately above the tower is Lee Dam, one of three tree-shrouded dams hovering above the hamlet and the scene of an annual New Year 'dip' - for the brave or foolhardy! Also prominent here is the Top Brink, a sprawling hostelry. Stoodley Pike monument is in view from the outset, but frustratingly seems to keep its distance!

From the pub descend either the enclosed setted path or the road by the old tower and head along the endlessly rising road. *En route note a sundial of 1864 on the corner of a cottage, complete with a 'time-rhyme'.* After a long three-quarters of a mile another pub, the Shepherd's Rest, is reached. Here take a gate on the left and follow a good track doubling steadily back up the moor. Almost at once a splendidly flagged packhorse route is crossed. Before long ignore a steeper right branch, keeping to the gentler left one to rise to some old workings. Now narrower but totally foolproof, the path rises ever gradually beneath the dark cliffs of Langfield Edge. *The edge bears shapely rock formations and the scars of long abandoned quarrying.* Your superb path is carried across successive embankments of two old dams beneath old quarries.

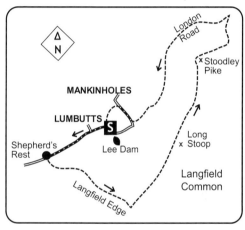

Eventually this splendidly engineered way gains the far end of the brooding rocks, then a path contours around the head of Black Clough and doubles back across the far side. *Throughout this moorland section savour vast, sweeping views across upper Calderdale, full of colour and interest in stark contrast to the flat moors to your right.* The path remains clear as it soon commences a gentle rise above a well-defined edge enhanced by a rash of boulders. As the slope tails off so do the rocks, and the path skirts the top of Coldwell Hill. The path then drops gently past a prominent cairn to merge with the unmistakable course of the Pennine Way. Bear left on its part-flagged course past a memorial seat on a slight drop before rising (ignore a lesser branch curving right) to a crossroads with a well-preserved paved way.

The junction is overseen by the Long Stoop, an old guidepost of monumental stature. *Here the modern foot traveller's highway, the Pennine Way, meets a centuries old packhorse route known (like several others) as the Long Causeway. The preserved section of flags can be seen going all the way down towards Mankinholes.* Your path advances straight on, rising through an old quarry and following a broad and popular course through clusters of rocks along to the Stoodley Pike monument. *Erected in 1815 to celebrate peace after victory over Napoleon, it later collapsed and was replaced by a new tower in 1856. An inscription over the door explains some of its history. It stands a mighty 120 feet above the 1312ft/400m moortop, and is the upper valley's most famous landmark. A dark, spiral staircase climbs 39 steps to a viewing balcony: the 360-degree panorama features moorland skylines in almost every direction, and a pleasing aspect is the way intervening slopes mask the industrialised valley floor.*

The Long Stoop   *Opposite: Stoodley Pike*

Leave the top with the Pennine Way striking eastwards. The broad path passes a spring bursting forth into a trough whose inscription 'public slake trough' now appears indiscernible. At a wall-gap the path receives a 'firming up'. It runs a few yards further with a wall to a gateway in it, then drops down below the Doe Stones. *Previous instructions regarding a sunken quarry track are now superfluous as the path has been so zealously upgraded.* Dropping onto a broad, level track at a crossroads with the Pennine Bridleway go left on it, and after passing through a gate it runs a largely level course beneath the Pike's steep slopes. This old track is known as London Road, and leads unfailingly along the foot of the common to eventually reach a corner. Keep straight on the walled track in front to drop down to the edge of Mankinholes. *This old handloom weaving settlement largely by-passed by the modern age has great water troughs as a sign of its importance in pack-horse days. Most visitors today are youth hostellers breaking their Pennine Way journey in the shadow of Stoodley Pike.*

Turn right through the hamlet to the last buildings, and on as far as a lone house. *This is the site of Mankinholes Methodist Church.* Here turn left down the splendidly paved Lumbutts Lane to return unfailingly to the start at Lumbutts. *At the very foot of the lane note an old guidepost inscribed 'Halifax' and 'Heptonstall', complete with mileages.*

JUMBLE HOLE CLOUGH

START *Lobb Mill   Grid ref. SD 956246*

DISTANCE *5^{1}2 miles (9km)*

ORDNANCE SURVEY MAPS
1:50,000
Landranger 103 - Blackburn & Burnley
1:25,000
Outdoor Leisure 21 - South Pennines

ACCESS *Start from Lobb Mill car park/picnic area 1^{1}2 miles east of Todmorden centre on the Hebden Bridge road. Served by Hebden Bridge-Todmorden bus.*

> *A labyrinth of hillside tracks and a towpath trod sandwich the highlight, a descent of fascinating Jumble Hole Clough*

Leave the car park by the path at its eastern end, rising across the breast of a hugely colourful pocket of open country. *Virtually from the outset you are treated to extensive views over the valley, to Stoodley Pike opposite and high moors east and west. Below, the railway disappears beneath you into Horsefall Tunnel.* As the green way zigzags up avoid any lesser forks, and at the top the path becomes enclosed to enter Rodwell, a hidden hamlet of character-ful old houses. Pass between them on the rough access road out, and at an early T-junction, turn left and remain on the same track to eventually rise to Cross Stone Road.

Turn right along the road for a couple of minutes and then left up Butts Lane between two houses. This climbs steeply past a small group of houses until turning sharply left and losing its surface at a lone dwelling: here go straight up a short enclosed way, through a small gate to a crossroads of ways. Turn right, immediately passing through a stile and on a path across to a small tree-lined stream. On emerging, forsake the thin trod ahead and jink left briefly uphill, then resume a level course passing above the confines of Higher Birks. On the other side is a choice of green ways: turn left up the sunken way engulfed in dry reeds. Rising gently between long-collapsed walls, it doubles back a little before levelling out.

At around 1050ft/320m this is the highest point of the walk. Note the complete disappearance of the busy valley floor: there is virtually no evidence that you are in industrial Calderdale, for the shelves of lush, walled pastures that characterise this part of the dale hide the deep valley bottom. The track runs on the field bottom as a splendid green way, becoming enclosed at the end to emerge onto a narrow road. Go left to a junction and then right to the prominent Great Rock. *This is aptly named, seeming all the more imposing for its roadside location. The too-accessible rock is festooned with untold carved initials and professions of undying love: scramble to the top and enjoy the view.*

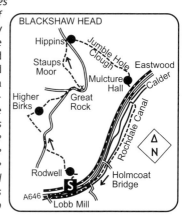

Leave the road by an enclosed grass track left of the rock. On emptying onto heathery Staups Moor it turns to descend by a wall, crossing a track and a ladder-stile into a reedy pasture to drop directly onto a road. Cross Hippins Bridge to turn immediately right on a short access track to Hippins. *Just along it is the lovely old house of dark millstone grit, with mullioned windows and sporting a 1656 datestone.* Immediately after the house take a kissing-gate to the right and follow a wallside path away. An early stile in it marks the point to branch off right, a path materialising to descend stone steps to a footbridge across the beck. Here begins the descent of Jumble Hole Clough: never too claustrophobic, it is sheer delight. *Note the delectable waterslide immediately downstream, and the line of the water-cut to supply Staups Mill.*

Turn downstream to the ruined Staups Mill. *This former cotton spinning mill occupies an evocative setting. Lower down you will see further remains of mills and associated workings, making it possible to visualise its industrial heyday: this little beck certainly paid its way.* Leaving the mill the path rises briefly, but part way up take a left fork to remain parallel with but high above the beck. After passing with care above a substantial crag the path descends steadily to cross an angled cross-paths and then along the edge of two fields, returning into the denser woods to merge into a descending farm drive. Just below an old millpond it doubles back to cross the beck, then clings to its other bank to run by mill ruins to arrive at Jumble Hole, overlooked by a tall red-brick chimney.

Immediately before the first houses cross a footbridge on the right and a little path runs into a field, tracing the right-hand wall up to a knoll. *On this delightful spot is a stone seat amid clumps of heather, and lovely views featuring the particularly dense woodland of the valley-side slopes. Through the wooded clough opposite, eyes are drawn to Stoodley Pike's noble sentinel on the lofty moorland skyline.* Continue on to a corner in front of Mulcture Hall, squeezing through into the garden top to join the hairpin of an access road. Turn down past the house, and at the next hairpin go right on a grassy path between trees and railway. Use the tall footbridge to cross the railway and return to the valley floor.

Dropping to the main road at Eastwood go right only a few strides before crossing to escape on Burnt Acres Lane over a river bridge alongside an old mill. *Yes, that was the elusive Calder.* Continue on to cross a canal bridge, then turn immediately right. *Easier still, you could simply join the towpath here.* Rising beneath an extended garden a path heads off into the trees, running a delightful course through the wood above the canal, making a fine alternative to the towpath. After a slight rise to an intervening wall-stile the path drops back to a road at Holmcoat Bridge and Lock: the towpath is rejoined here. During the next mile you pass three locks, an odd mill, and an interesting island-like section between canal and river. *For a note on the Rochdale Canal see page 49.* Another road is crossed at Shawplains Lock, and you leave the towpath on reaching the lock and road bridge at Lobb Mill. *The mill itself was demolished long ago.* Turn to rejoin the main road opposite a viaduct and right again to rapidly return to the start.

WITHENS CLOUGH

START *Cragg Vale   Grid ref. SD 999231*

DISTANCE *6 miles (9¹2km)*

ORDNANCE SURVEY MAPS
1:50,000
Landranger 103 - Blackburn & Burnley
Landranger 104 - Leeds, Bradford & Harrogate
1:25,000
Explorer OL21 - South Pennines

ACCESS *Start from the church, just beneath the main road (signed Church Bank Lane). Roadside parking. Served by bus from Hebden Bridge via Mytholmroyd. •ACCESS NOTE: Open Access, see page 8, some water company permissive paths, all within Access Land.*

Splendid beck scenery precedes a climb to breezy moorland with wonderful views and a host of fine features

Cragg Vale's claim to infamy is as the home of the Yorkshire Coiners. It is the most romantically recalled (though far from only) site of 18th century counterfeiting: the practice involved clipping gold from guineas to make additional, inferior coins. Cragg Vale's bleak moorland beginnings soon transform into a deep, richly-wooded valley before joining the Calder Valley at Mytholmroyd. The first and last stages of the walk shadow Cragg Brook through fascinating terrain with reminders of the mills it was made to serve. The sombre church of St John the Baptist in the Wilderness dates from 1840, with the Hinchliffe Arms in its shadow.

From the pub advance very briefly along the cul-de-sac clough road, quickly turning left at a surfaced drive climbing away. From a stile at the end of the grounds on the left a broad path crosses to a gate, from where a thinner path runs away, bearing left to the edge of a small wood. It runs on the wood edge to emerge over-looking Cragg Brook. Advance on, ignoring a lower fork to the brook and rising along the wood edge to quickly enter comprehensive woodland. A superb stride rises steadily and runs high above the stream, and just after a branch drops left, your way is ushered down by a wall to a stile alongside the brook. Enclosed by a wall a path then runs upstream the short way to a clapper-bridge on the brook. Ignoring the fork that crosses it, instead pass through a small gate in the adjacent wall. Here begins a steep wallside ascent of colourful country aided by a fair portion of stone steps. Easing out at the top with a ruin to the left, pass through an old gateway and a broader way slants gently right up towards Higher House.

Don't enter, but level with the house take a path heading away to the left, quickly rising slightly to a stile onto the foot of the largely grassy Turley Holes & Higher House Moor. Go right on what proves a grand path by

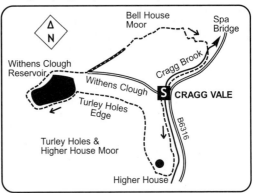

a ditch, rising slightly along the moor edge above woodland. Crossing a brow it drops very slightly to reveal Withens Clough below, with richly-wooded Cragg Vale leading away. Before the slope steepens you meet the end of a catchwater drain: turn left on a superb grassy path tracing its level course all the way along Turley Holes Edge to Withens Clough Reservoir, whose dam soon appears ahead. *It was completed in 1894 for Morley Corporation.*

For a short-cut simply cross the dam, otherwise resume on the shore, a path quickly bridging a drain to run a grand embanked course alongside the reservoir shore. This leads unfailingly to the head and around to a gate onto the start of a firm track. Turn right on this to quickly return as a walled way outside the reservoir wall, passing the old keeper's house to reach the northern end of the dam. *From here a surfaced road drops back down to the start for a quick finish.* For the full walk take the access road rising left from the car park. This long, steady slant uphill eases out alongside a wood, and runs on to a fork. Take the right-hand level branch, a rougher access road that remains enclosed before opening out beneath a corner of Bell House Moor. *Massive views look out over Cragg Vale.*

Just short of the house at High Green, take a gate set slightly back to the right. Descend a part sunken way to a wall below, then drop left with it to a stile at the end. Head away on an enclosed grass path beneath enclosures of assorted livestock, emerging at the end into the right-hand field via a makeshift gate. Cross to a gate/stile opposite, then bear right to drop to a very isolated house in front of woods. Bear right of it to a stile, then down outside it to a corner stile onto the foot of an enclosed green way. Go right, a path now bearing right to slant down a part wooded enclosure to a stile in the corner. *More open views look over Cragg Vale.*

Drop down the wallside below, using a stile near the bottom to cross and slant down to the top of a wooded bank. Here you join a clear path running above dense hollies. Go right, soon slanting left down above the denser scrub. Quickly emerging into more open surrounds, double back left and spiral down briefly more steeply to a fence corner below. A nicer green way slants left beneath the fence to a stile at the corner, where the path forks. Go right, a thin trod doubling back down beneath a low bank to a gate in the bottom corner above the wooded environs of Cragg Brook. A broad path drops right to a gate to emerge alongside Papermill Cottage and old mill ruins.

Cross the bridge in front and ignore the access road rising left, instead turning right up a firm path beneath a house. This rises up and on to an access road at houses at Castlegate Mill. *The Robin Hood pub is just along to the left.* Bear right on this, and though you could remain on it to a stone-arched bridge at the end, a nicer variant drops down steps to a millpond below, and a good path runs along its far bank through grand woodland, rejoining the road just short of the bridge. Don't cross it but take a gate/stile to run upstream through two open pastures, the part-kerbed green path crossing to a bridle-gate at the end into a yard of tall buildings with the church just behind. Rise up the short drive and along to finish.

BLACKSTONE EDGE

START Windy Hill   Grid ref. SD 982141

DISTANCE 6¹⁄4 miles (10km)

ORDNANCE SURVEY MAPS
1:50,000
Landranger 109 - Manchester
1:25,000
Explorer OL21 - South Pennines

ACCESS Start from a large roadside parking area amid boundary signs by the large mast just above Junction 22 of the M62. Served by Halifax-Rochdale bus. •ACCESS NOTE: Open Access, see page 8. The entire walk is on rights of way and water company permissive paths within Open Access land.

A bracing walk through archetypal South Pennine moorland to a landmark crest, much of it on easy paths and tracks

Despite the moorland remoteness of this walk, the dominant feature is the presence of the hand of man, be it reservoir, pylon, motorway, Roman road, packway, mast, windfarm, ... Also novel is the starting altitude at an appropriately blustery 1368ft/417m! A more historic Lancashire boundary stone stands amid modern signs. From the outset Blackstone Edge beckons ahead beyond the mast. From the parking area follow the firm course of the Pennine Way northwards, crossing the mast access road and dropping down to quickly reach and cross the Pennine Way footbridge. You are now the highest person in the country 'on' a motorway. Bear left on the stony path rising to a cairned knoll, then on to a bridle-gate in a fence. The path swings around to the right to replace the M62 with the prospect of waiting Blackstone Edge, a fair deal! The restored path makes light work of the peat bogs of Redmires as it rises towards the edge. *Green Withens Reservoir appears in its entirety down to the right, you will later return along its embankment.* With the bouldery crest of the edge straight ahead, the path leads unerringly to its top. The edge itself actually forms well before the cairned path reaches it, and many obviously gain it a little earlier.

At 1548ft/472m the highest point is not in doubt, as an Ordnance Survey column is cemented to a mighty boulder. The highest point in this collection of Calderdale walks enjoys outstanding views, though perhaps the finest feature is the rocky edge itself. Westwards you look down on a great spread of greater Manchester beyond Littleborough and Hollingworth Lake. The Summit Gorge is backed by Scout Moor windfarm, and leads the eye to Coal Clough windfarm and Pendle Hill through the Cliviger Gorge, while to the north Black Hameldon and Boulsworth Hill lead round to Ovenden Moor windfarm. Did I just say windfarm? Southwards, meanwhile, are the high moors of the Dark Peak. The finest climbing ground amongst what is otherwise largely scrambling opportunities is found towards the northern limits of the edge, and set a short way down the slope: this proves to be a massive cliff with bold faces and interesting chimneys.

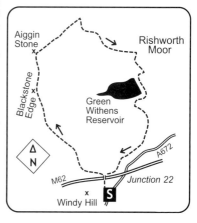

Resume northwards along the edge path, soon crossing more modest stony ground to a stile admitting onto a path junction at the Aiggin Stone. *This is a junction of once-important packhorse routes, where Rochdale-Halifax and Oldham-Burnley trails met. The old guidestone has been restored, and remarkably there is more of it below ground than above. Further down the Lancashire side is a superb surviving cobbled section, long attributed to the Romans but probably dating from packhorse times.* Turn right, the path immediately crossing the brow and soon shaking off the fence.

A gradual descent begins on a broad, distinctive part-sunken way, a little peaty in parts. *There is a glimpse of Baitings Reservoir beneath Great Manshead Hill.* The path drops down to a bridge on the concrete Rishworth Drain, across which is a path crossroads.

Turn right on the level drain-side path, quickly curving left to absorb a grassy path coming in from the left. *This 'nick' in the moor reveals the motorway and the moors to the south joining the Windy Hill mast.* Just ahead the Rishworth Drain goes off right, but your path bears left alongside a reedy channel. *Green Withens Reservoir appears below with the knobbly crest of Blackstone Edge above.* The way runs pleasantly on towards Green Withens Edge, the point of departure coming at the sudden end of the drain. While a path rises straight on, the main path turns down the moor, merges with another from the right, then bears left through reedy terrain to a wide bridge over another major drain. Turn right on the broad track to quickly reach the dam of Green Withens Reservoir.

A grassy stroll above the rough road along the dam leads round to a derelict building on the other side. *All the while, Blackstone Edge still features prominently across the rising moor beyond the head of the reservoir. Green Withens Reservoir was completed in 1898 by Wakefield Corporation, and enlarged in 1925.* At the track junction go left on the main drive out, yet again with a drain for company. When the reservoir road turns off for the main road, keep right on a green track by the drain to reach its terminus at a basin under the motorway fence. A broad path turns up its side to quickly return to the motorway footbridge, to conclude as you began.

The bouldery crest of Blackstone Edge

17

RISHWORTH MOOR

START *Oxygrains Bridge   Grid ref. SE 003158*

DISTANCE *5¹4 miles (8¹2km)*

ORDNANCE SURVEY MAPS
1:50,000
Landranger 109 - Manchester
Landranger 110 - Sheffield & Huddersfield
1:25,000
Explorer OL21 - South Pennines

ACCESS *Start from the A672 Oldham road from Ripponden midway between it gaining the open moor west of the Turnpike Inn, and Junction 22 of the M62. Parking area alongside the bridge. Served by Halifax-Oldham bus. •ACCESS NOTE: Open Access, see page 8. Some water company permissive paths on Open Access land.*

An invigorating ramble over archetypal grassy Pennine moorland

Oxygrains Bridge is a large structure that entirely dwarves Oxygrains Old Bridge, an outstanding packhorse bridge at the confluence just below you. From the parking area cross the road (not the bridge) to a bridle-gate in a fence: a splendid green path heads up the valley of Oxygrains. *This largely follows the course of a 3¹2ft gauge railway that ran up Green Withens Clough to transport quarried stone for the building of Green Withens Reservoir.* At a knoll the valley in front proves to be merely the side valley of Wolden Edge Clough, and your main one is revealed striking away to the right. The path runs on to the rugged environs of Castle Dean Rocks: a fork here sees a lower path remain by the stream, but the main one slants right up to a knoll. Just a few strides to your left is a delightful grassy sward above an imposing cliff. *This makes a grand spot to linger, but be wary of the exposed situation.*

The path resumes by swinging round with the beck through Green Withens Clough to see the dam of Green Withens Reservoir high in front, backed by Blackstone Edge. After crossing a side clough the path runs a distinct level course free of bracken to a gateway in a wall just short of the dam, then slants right up alongside an outflow to emerge at its northern end. *Completed in 1898 by Wakefield Corporation, the reservoir was enlarged in 1925.* Turn right along the unsurfaced reservoir road, which swings sharp right to follow the broad Green Withens Drain away beneath Green Withens Edge. Already, by the first bridge, your objective of the pronounced Whinny Nick can be discerned on the skyline ahead.

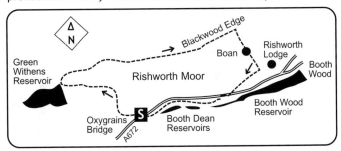

Becoming less firm, it is only vacated upon reaching the fourth bridge since joining it. Across it a rough track climbs away, but within a few strides bear right on a more inviting thin path. This slants gently up through bracken to quickly emerge onto the open, higher reaches of Rishworth Moor. Beyond a tiny stream crossing, it continues slanting to reveal the conspicuous Whinny Nick ahead. It now runs a largely level course, joining an old sunken way to rise to the distinct groove marked by a cairn/stake and a rash of stones. At some 1350ft/412m this is the highest point of the walk. From here the view eastwards opens up, and it is this direction you take, by keeping higher ground to the left and following a clear path, descending imperceptibly across the extensive moor.

The path continues past a few piles of stones at a small quarry site from where it is accompanied by a faint reedy ditch. This arrangement is kept as slopes to the left diminish to reveal a wide view to the north as you gain the north side of this broad moorland tongue. The way now bears right to traverse the better-defined

Blackwood Edge. *Extensive views look north over Ripponden and the Ryburn Valley, with Ovenden Moor windfarm on the skyline beyond. Blackwood Edge Road, which you are travelling, serviced the moorland quarries: its name is an indication that it once saw rather more use than today!* As the drain finally drops away the path contours above the steeper drop to reach a tall ladder-stile in an intervening wall which should have been visible well in advance.

While the sunken way heads through a gate by the stile, don't cross but turn right on a path over the immediate brow. Veering slightly right to a stile halfway along a facing wall, it can be easily missed as the main path bears further right of it. Descend a green pasture to a ladder-stile on the right side of farm buildings at Boan, then join its drive to drop to a sharp bend left. From a gate on the right a grassy cart-track heads away past a stand of trees into rough pasture, then becomes enclosed by walls to slant down to a gate/stile onto a bracken-clad corner of the moor. As a firmer track it slants down past a stone shed to rejoin the road at old quarries.

Turn right on the verge, with the great cliffs of Derby Delph directly below. *A delph was a quarry, and here stone for Green Withens Reservoir was won.* Immediately after the wall enclosing the quarry ends a guidepost sends a path branching off left. Though narrow, it runs a clear, near-level course along a slender, bracken-clad strip between Booth Dean and the road above. Below is the very upper reach of Booth Wood Reservoir. *With its mighty dam almost a mile down valley, the 50-acre reservoir was completed in 1971.* Lower and Upper Booth Dean Reservoirs immediately upstream are very slender and attractive neighbours, built in 1923 to supply Wakefield: beyond the last reservoir the path rises back onto the road at the start.

Castle Dean Rocks, Oxygrains

BLACK BROOK

START *Stainland   Grid ref. SE 078195*

DISTANCE *5 miles (8km)*

ORDNANCE SURVEY MAPS
1:50,000
Landranger 104 - Leeds, Bradford & Harrogate
Landranger 110 - Sheffield & Huddersfield
1:25,000
Explorer OL21 - South Pennines

ACCESS *Start from the village centre, car park on main street. Served by Halifax-Elland-Huddersfield bus, or direct from Halifax.*

> *A lively exploration of the unsung side valley, with the ancient settlement of Barkisland midway*

Stainland is a hilltop village equidistant from Halifax and Huddersfield: several of its features are mentioned at the start and finish of the route. Head eastwards down the main street a short way and turn left on Drury Lane opposite the Duke of York pub, just a few strides after attractive Holroyd Square. *Beginning as a cobbled street, Drury Lane was made for carting stone from the quarries at its other end.* Beyond some cottages it continues as a good walled path between fields, at the end emerging onto a colourful brow above a line of old quarries at Eaves Top. *This is a splendid viewpoint, looking over the great sprawl of Halifax and its neighbourhood.* Go left on the main track slanting down onto a grassy shelf beneath large quarried cliffs.

Just short of an enormous free-standing boulder, a thin path doubles back right, rapidly becoming distinct to slant down a bank between old walls. Within a minute it drops left to descend a colourful bank to the top of a golf course. Go straight down, passing right of a large clump of trees and down to the nearest trees below. A path drops through them to escape the course at a hidden tee. Continue down the wooded bank to a stile into a field. A thin path drops to the bottom to emerge by a row of houses in the shadow of a derelict mill at Gate Head. Cross the bridge beyond and turn immediately upstream on a path shadowing Black Brook. Remain with the brook to approach Bowers Mill, bearing slightly right to a gate into the yard. Keep straight on through the buildings and up the access road at the end to join Branch Road.

Go left on the footway until just past a bend: cross to a narrow stile on the right immediately after a lone house, and after its garden wall ends a nice little path bears right to the top corner of the field. From the stile head straight

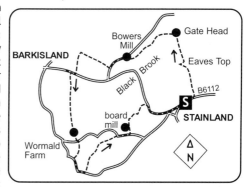

up the side of tree-lined Sandyfoot Clough, a grand climb that only ends when there appears no obvious way ahead. Cross a stile in the adjacent fence and rise up by a crumbling wall to a wall corner above. To avoid exuberant stinging vegetation pass between a red-brick structure and the wall to enter a walled grass track. At the end don't go right into modern housing, but take small gates in front to enter the grounds of Barkisland Hall. *This is a real gem, dating from 1638 and boasting a magnificent three-storey front.* Advance parallel with its short drive to a gate out onto Stainland Road at the foot of Barkisland. Turn up into the main street of this characterful village: your point of departure is a narrow stile on the left alongside the village stocks. Just a little further up the street, however, are the rather splendid Nolson House and then the Griffin Inn, both on the right.

Departing, a short snicket leaves the stile to enter a field. Descend with an old wall to Barkisland Clough, crossing a single slab bridge and up the other bank to stone steps out of the trees. *Good open views look down to the left, and back over Barkisland.* Head away with the wall along to an old green lane. Cross straight over, now with a wall on the right. At the end pass through a line of trees to resume with another wall just ahead. From the stile at the end, bear left to the far corner in front of Wormald Farm: a gate puts you into the yard. *Pause to admire the beautiful old house with its mullioned and transomed windows and a 1694 date-stone on the porch.* Opposite the house, leave the drive by a stile on the left and cross the field to the wooded top of Bottomley Clough.

A stile admits onto a road: go left a few strides then take a stile on the right. At the field-end cross to a stile ahead then keep straight on along the bottom of several narrow fields linked by stiles. At the end a longer field leads on to join a short drive beneath houses, out onto Steel Lane. Turn steeply downhill past houses at Penny Hill, and at the second sharp, cobbled bend go left on a path into scrubby undergrowth. Moderately claustrophobic in late summer, it slowly improves to slant briefly up to a stile in the corner. Cross a slim enclosure above new woodland to the isolated house at Crow Wood. Pass beneath it to a gate at the other side, joining its drive. *Stainland sits on the hillside opposite.* As Crow Wood Lane this runs a delightful course down to emerge onto another hairpin bend. Turn down above a millpond to the valley floor, occupied by a vast board mill. Starting to rise away, turn left at the first chance on an access road on the top side of the mill.

Just before the road turns left, take an inviting path doubling back right just before the actual footpath sign! This old way rises into the trees and enjoys a superb zigzag climb through the wood, partly between old walls, to emerge up a short walled way at the top. Go left on the wallside to a gate/stile onto the foot of an access road (Broad Royd), and turn up past the short terrace to join Beestonley Lane. Go right up the footway to re-enter Stainland. *Views over to the right lead up the Black Brook valley to the M62 crossing the Scammonden dam. En route the massive former Providence Chapel of 1814 is passed.* Keep on, bearing left at a couple of junctions in the village to return to the start. *On the first of these the house on the left corner at Well Royd bears a 1762 datestone. Several pubs are passed, along with an imposing former chapel of 1883 and the old farmhouse of Ellistones.*

19

GREAT MANSHEAD HILL

START Baitings   Grid ref. SE 012190

DISTANCE $5^3$4 miles (9km)

ORDNANCE SURVEY MAPS
1:50,000
Landranger 103 - Blackburn & Burnley
Landranger 104 - Leeds, Bradford & Harrogate
Landranger 109 - Manchester
Landranger 110 - Sheffield & Huddersfield
1:25,000
Explorer OL21 - South Pennines

ACCESS Start from a water company car park at Baitings Reservoir on the A58 west of Ripponden. Served by Halifax-Rochdale bus. •ACCESS NOTE: Open Access, see page 8. Permissive paths by Baitings Reservoir and onto Manshead Hill.

> *A richly varied walk dominated by a splendid moorland crossing of a magnificent viewpoint*

Baitings Reservoir was completed in 1956 on the site of a smaller dam dating from the 1920s. It now fills a vast area of the broader, upper reaches of the Ryburn Valley. The massive concrete dam might rapidly induce vertigo, being curiously sinuous and with unusually low walls. Hold on to your false teeth if brave enough to peer over it! The roadside house was until recent times the New Inn: it displays an interesting large sundial. Cross the dam and turn immediately right through a kissing-gate, from where a permissive path runs through trees, becoming clearer as it quickly joins the reservoir shore. *Shapely Manshead End projects itself invitingly across the waters.* This pleasant, easy start runs the length of the reservoir to emerge through denser woodland onto a road.

Turn right over Baitings Viaduct to bridge the upper reach of the reservoir. *From it, in times of low water levels, the bridge and old road that ran above the original reservoir are revealed.* The road then rises to join the A58. Cross to a footway and go left past a junction with Blue Ball Road, then within a minute take a ladder-stile on the right at the start of the permissive path up Manshead End. The path drops to bridge a tiny stream then rises to a fence to work its way up the side of Greenwood Clough. Passing left of the renovated farm at Manshead, it curves left with a wall to re-cross the stream (simple bridge) and rise through an old wall. Part way up the rough enclosure pass through a gap in the crumbling wall to a stile in the parallel fence. The initially faint but improving path now rises over open rough moor, aided by occasional marker posts.

Keep right at a moist area and soon the upper reach of the clough is re-crossed (plank bridge) and an old wall is passed through to another parallel fence-stile. From here the grand little path forsakes the fence to rise up to the waiting edge of Manshead End. The final pull is a short, stiff one up to the cairn.

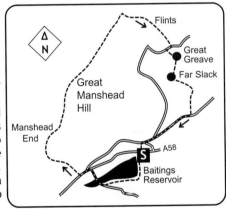

This is the finest moment of the walk, certainly on a clear day, and the modest rash of stones makes a splendid refreshment halt: a wooden bench even sits just to the right. Ignore the path forking right, past the bench, and advance on the one to a shelter cairn and an OS column just a little further. *At 1368ft/417m this is the summit of Great Manshead Hill, with a superb all-round panorama. Westwards is layer upon layer of rolling moorland, from across the Summit Gorge round to Stoodley Pike monument, Coal Clough windfarm on the Long Causeway, the Gorple and Widdop moors, Ovenden Moor windfarm, Norland Moor, and then round by way of*

Emley Moor TV mast behind Ringstone Edge Reservoir towards Baitings Reservoir, with the moors beyond supporting Holme Moss TV mast at the northern limits of the Peak District National Park.

The clear path continues north along the hill, keeping slightly left of the watershed and entering tracts of heather. *This brings views down into the colourful upper reaches of Cragg Vale. Ahead, Sowerby Bridge adds an urban touch.* Eventually a wall comes in below, and the path drops to join a grassy track alongside it. *The first of several 'S B' boundary stones within the next half-mile is passed.* Through a gate/stile where a fence takes over, continue on to a crossroads of grassy tracks. *Distinctive hummocks hereabouts are the remains of old slate quarries.* Turn right here past a red-brick ruin. *This is part of the scant remains of a wartime decoy site, intended to confuse German bombers.* Dropping gently down to a wall-corner, leave by a stile in it. The path is guided across a rough enclosure to a stile at a fence corner at the corner of the old Flint Reservoir, then runs along the right-hand minor embankment to join a farm road at a bend. Turn right down this, soon becoming fully enclosed to emerge onto a narrow road.

Go right for a minute and down the first drive. At the bend, go straight through the big gates into the yard of Great Greave. *This grand house dates from the early 17th century, its hidden frontage boasting two gables, mullioned windows and a superb outlook.* Pass round to the right and without going to the front, turn through a small gate by a shed and descend an old walled way. It drops to a stile at the bottom into the minor Blackshaw Clough. A faint way rises up the curving wallside opposite. At the gate/stile above, turn to admire Great Greave, then continue along the wallside to Far Slack Farm. Squeeze through a gap left of the first building to emerge into the yard, and follow the drive out for some way. At a T-junction of tracks at the next house, double back right up a more inviting walled green way, winding pleasantly up to emerge onto a road. Turn right for a good three-quarters of a mile to reach a large, isolated house. *Until about 2002 this was the Blue Ball Inn. Its reputation for good ales wasn't enough to save this old pack-horse inn serving the route out of Lancashire over Blackstone Edge proper. All that remains is its view over the dam to Rishworth Moor.* Here leave the road by a path descending the side of a small unkempt pasture back onto the A58 opposite the car park.

UPPER RYBURN

START *Ripponden* *Grid ref. SE 040197*

DISTANCE *5³4 miles (9km)*

ORDNANCE SURVEY MAPS
1:50,000
Landranger 104 - Leeds, Bradford & Harrogate
Landranger 110 - Sheffield & Huddersfield
1:25,000
Explorer OL21 - South Pennines

ACCESS *Start from the parish church in the centre. Car park just above, across the main road. Served by bus from Halifax via Sowerby Bridge, many continuing to Rochdale and Oldham.*

> *An intimate exploration of the upper reaches of the Ryburn Valley, returning along quiet roads and green lanes*

Ripponden is a busy village, its old centre being a conservation area. Here is St Bartholomew's church, its spire reaching to the heavens, while alongside is a restored packhorse bridge. The white-walled and even more historic Old Bridge Inn is only one of several pubs. The railway arrived from Sowerby Bridge in 1881 and closed in 1958: sections of it are put to use as permissive paths.

From the church do not cross either of the bridges, but pass between the houses at Bridge End and underneath the main road bridge over the Ryburn. A cobbled road heads upstream, then pass through a small park onto a road. Advance along this, and beyond the houses and small industrial estate a surfaced drive runs along the riverbank. When this ends at Ellis Bottom Farm a path takes over to trace the Ryburn to a footbridge. Don't cross, but take a few stone steps up to resume through the trees. Ignore too a branch left up to an old bridge over the former railway. The path drops back to the river and along above a perilously steep plunge to the river to reach its confluence with Booth Dean Beck. *This woodland section is superb: across the river you pass several mills that have been transformed to residential use, though several weirs testify to the traditional mill needs of times past: the most action they see today is a heron taking flight.*

Just to the left cross the inflowing beck and up short-lived Holme House Lane onto the A672, using that to cross the Ryburn itself before departing immediately left on Bar Lane, parallel with the river. This runs upstream to an eventual demise at some new housing. En route much housing is passed, then a charming mill-pond on the left and an almost hidden one on the right. *The new housing is on the site of a former mill: latterly a paper mill, a nice touch into the 1990s was a quaint fire appliance in its own garage.*

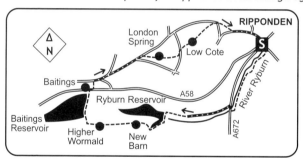

A cobbled road takes over to climb to a hairpin bend. Here go straight ahead round to the left of a garage, where a path is found with a millpond below and the curved concrete dam of Ryburn Reservoir dramatically in front. Reaching a junction continue up ahead to quickly emerge at a car park at the dam's north end. *Ryburn Reservoir was built for Wakefield Corporation, and largely surrounded by woodland, it blends well in its deeper fold of the valley. This is in contrast to its more recent neighbour, whose dam is visible ahead. Beneath Ryburn's dam compare 'progress' in water conservation, with the old millpond overshadowed by the hundred foot high dam.*

Cross the dam and take the broad path right, above the water's edge to reach a footbridge over the head of the reservoir's southern arm. Across it a path climbs through trees to a stile into a field, then rises by a wall to become enclosed before arriving at New Barn Farm. An enclosed path passes right of the buildings and directly along the field behind, rising in a straight line before it levels out to run to a stile. *Across to the left is the wide span of Rishworth Moor, with the drone of the unseen M62 motorway sometimes coming from beyond it. Baitings Dam now re-appears beneath Manshead End.* Continue along this pleasant crest, soon becoming enclosed again and along to a path junction where the old way swings up to the left. Take the small gate on the right into a field containing the ruin of New House just down to the right. *The upper reach of Ryburn Reservoir is seen down to the right.*

From the wall corner by the ruin an old way runs left, rising gently with a wall in the direction of Baitings Reservoir. It soon becomes enclosed to run pleasantly on to the house at Higher Wormald, with a 1796 datestone. At the end don't follow the drive rising away, but take a kissing-gate by the outhouse on the right to cross two fields to Upper Schole Carr Farm. Here turn right down a track to cross the dam of Baitings Reservoir. *This was completed as recently as 1956 on the site of a much smaller reservoir dating from the 1920s. The massive concrete dam might rapidly induce vertigo, being curiously sinuous and with unusually low walls. Hold on to your false teeth if peering over it!*

Across the dam cross a car park to join the A58. *The house here was, until quite recently, the well-sited New Inn. All that remains is the interesting appendage of a large sundial.* From a stile opposite a path climbs the side of a small unkempt pasture to the parallel Blue Ball Road. *Disaster strikes again here as the house in front was, again until recently, the once very popular Blue Ball Inn. Its reputation for its choice of good ales wasn't enough to save this old packhorse inn serving the route out of Lancashire over Blackstone Edge proper. This was superseded by the modern turn-pike road over Blackstone Edge which adopted the lower route by what was the Blue Ball's suitable named lower neighbour. All that remains is its extensive view over the dam to Rishworth Moor.*

Turn right along the quiet, level road (avoiding lesser turns) for a good three-quarters of a mile. *This return walk has good views over to Norland Moor and down the Ryburn to Sowerby Bridge, where it meets the Calder.* At a crossroads with rough lanes just beyond a T-junction, go right on the walled track known as London Spring Road. Continue straight past the house at London Spring Farm, becoming a nicer track passing a pocket moor before running on to another road, Green Lane.

Go left just a few yards before branching right down another walled track. This is Cote Road, and soon on the left you pass the splendid old house of Low Cote, with its mullioned windows and dainty gabled porch. Further along, a firm driveway comes in to run on to another road. *Two minutes along to the right is the Beehive Inn, though Ripponden itself is only ten minutes away now.* Cross straight over behind a house, over a second road and along a green track. Just past a house, bear right down a wallside, quickly becoming tightly enclosed as a narrow green path descends between walls onto similarly narrow Royd Lane at a pleasant row of cottages. *A 1764 datestone adorns the next house down.* Royd Lane leads steeply and rapidly down into the centre of Ripponden. For the parish church cross straight over the main road and down a short lane to the packhorse bridge and pub.

The Old Bridge Inn, Ripponden

NORLAND MOOR

START Norland   Grid ref. SE 065224

DISTANCE 6 miles (9$\frac{1}{2}$km)

ORDNANCE SURVEY MAPS
1:50,000
Landranger 104 - Leeds, Bradford & Harrogate
1:25,000
Explorer OL21 - South Pennines

ACCESS Start from the crossroads of Shaw Lane, Clough Road and Berry Moor Road, by the war memorial. A car park hides just off Shaw Lane, by a children's play area on a corner of the moor. Served by bus from Halifax via Greetland.

> *A stroll round a popular local haunt: colourful surroundings, wide views and a wealth of interest*

Scattered Norland 'Town' is an isolated hilltop settlement boasting splendid clothiers' houses of centuries past: some are revealed later. St Luke's church, a school and a fine old milestone are all centrally placed, while opposite the car park a three-storey house bears a 1743 datestone. Of greater relevance at the outset is Norland Moor, an island-like heather tract perched high above Sowerby Bridge and the Ryburn Valley. It bears the much-healed scars of extensive small-scale quarrying, notably along the moor's western escarpment.

From the car park take the broad path rising diagonally away to the heathery old quarries on the brow. Forking within 50 strides, keep left to rise to a crossroads with a broader path. Turn right to rise very gently across the moor, passing above old quarry sites and along a gentle but obvious edge. Beyond a covered reservoir where the Calderdale Way departs left, the more extensive quarries of

Turgate Delph are passed, all totally reclaimed by the heather. *Just below on the roadside is the Moorcock Inn.* Forging on above the quarries, the main path bears left to the white-painted Ordnance Survey column at 931ft/284m. At the junction here turn right to regain the edge at the prominent Ladstone Rock. *This gritstone outcrop is a distinctive landmark with extensive views westwards over the Ryburn Valley featuring Crow Hill, Great Manshead Hill, Rishworth Moor, Blackstone Edge and the moors south of the M62.*

Resuming along the edge, the path soon drops towards the road. Without actually setting foot on tarmac however, advance straight on a parallel path to the very corner of the moor. Here take a clear path rising left to remain on the moor edge, rising by a wall, then gently veering away from it to a path junction at

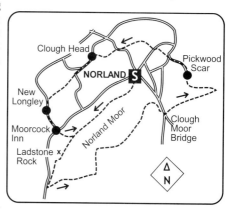

an outer wall corner. Now bear right on the splendid wallside path, enjoying a very gentle decline through hugely colourful vegetation. Reaching another corner an enclosed way runs straight on, but you go left to remain on the moor. Initially between walls, it then drops slightly to another outer corner. At this path crossroads go right to resume as before, on a broader path again gently declining. Ignore a branch left and remain on the path near the edge, curving round to the left to absorb the Calderdale Way at a solid cairn. *Ahead, the Wainhouse Tower gains in prominence, completely dwarfing the mill chimneys and church spires. This famous landmark was built in the 1870s to serve a dyeworks, and is usually open for ascents on public holidays.*

Keep on to the wall corner near the edge of the moor. At this crossroads, under a pylon, turn right to a road junction at Clough Moor Bridge. *An old boundary stone is set into the bridge,*

77

inscribed 'Division of Norland and Elland'. Cross the bridge, advance a few strides and take a stile on the left to immediately regain moorland. A thin path runs briefly left then turns downstream into quickly forming Maple Dean Clough, a riot of colourful vegetation. After crossing and re-crossing, the bottom of the wood proper is reached and the path runs along through trees to the right. When the accompanying fence turns away, the path drops a little to run on a level shelf into a break beneath overhead wires.

A lesser branch slants uphill but yours continues on, slanting into stately beeches to approach the rear of an isolated house. Here bear down to the left, where a thin path runs between hollies onto a level path at a bridle-gate. Go left on this largely flagged path along the base of the wood. The flags remain evident as the path runs on to a footbridge over the clough. An enclosed, setted path rises away, broadening into a track to reach the road end at the hamlet of Pickwood Scar. Head right on the road out, reaching a junction at a house. Here a flight of steps on the left sends a short, setted path up to a stile. The path climbs the field to another stile, then slants faintly across to a gate/stile in the corner above. A green lane runs the few strides right onto a road. *Outstanding just down to the right is Lower Old Hall, with a 1634 datestone and a two-storey porch.*

Turn briefly left to the former Blue Ball Inn. *A little higher up is Fallingworth Hall, dating from 1642 with mullioned windows*

and another two-storey porch. For a quick finish go to the junction above and turn right along Berry Moor Road. The main route takes a stile at the far end of the old pub, and heads away with a wallside to a path junction. Turn left here alongside an old vaccary wall. *A vaccary was a cattle farm. You now enjoy super views over Sowerby Bridge and up the valley.* At the end cross a walled green way and advance on, briefly enclosed, the route largely obvious as you pass through old stiles and along a field top. From a small gate at the end cross a field centre to a stile onto a road above Sowerby Croft.

Go briefly right to a kissing-gate opposite and a faint old way heads away along the field-top: Norland Moor appears above now. The path soon swings down to a corner stile, where a flagged path curves round a field bottom into an open area. Take the right fork, straight on into trees to emerge on Harper Royd Lane alongside a terrace at Clough Head. Go left on Hob Lane to rise past The Hobbit hotel. Ignore a right fork just past it and up a little further towards a bend, where bear right on an enclosed flagged path. Emerging into a field it bears left along the top, maintaining a direct line with largely flagged sections along fieldsides to emerge onto New Longley Lane above an old house, East Longley. Climb left past the intriguing terrace of New Longley to a T-junction at the Moorcock Inn. Cross to a parking area from where an old quarrymens' path slants left up onto the moor, passing between old quarries to meet the edge path of your outward route. Turn left to retrace opening steps back to the start.

Opposite: Milestone, Norland   ***Winter at Ladstone Rock***

CRAGG VALE

START Mytholmroyd   Grid ref. SE 012259

DISTANCE 6 miles ($9^1$2km)

ORDNANCE SURVEY MAPS
1:50,000
Landranger 103 - Blackburn & Burnley
Landranger 104 - Leeds, Bradford & Harrogate
1:25,000
Explorer OL21 - South Pennines

ACCESS Start from the village centre. Small car park over the bridge at the T-junction. Served by Halifax-Hebden Bridge bus and train.

A moderately strenuous but outstanding walk around lower Cragg Vale, over-riding feature being its many wooded delights

Mytholmroyd sprang up with the textile mills, and now large pockets of modern housing extend on both sides of the valley. St Michael's church stands just across the river, where the side valley of Cragg Brook joins the Calder. Such is the reputation of the local dock leaves that Mytholmroyd is home of a restored tradition, the World Dock Pudding Championship. Cross the bridge on the B6138, along New Road passing under the railway bridge. *On the left is a modern Roman Catholic church.* Opposite the Shoulder of Mutton (note the mounting steps) bear left on Scout Road. *Just on the left stands an old house with mullioned windows.* At once turn sharply right up Hall Bank Lane at the side of the Methodist Church.

Remain on the steeply climbing lane to make a quick exit from town to country. *Free of houses you can look over Mytholmroyd to the moors behind. Heptonstall church tower is conspicuous on the skyline, while Bell House Moor and Broadhead Clough impress over Cragg Vale, more so as the walk progresses.* The road winds up to suddenly end as a drive goes left. Your continuation of Stake Lane is the enclosed path ahead, climbing partly flagged and through colourful vegetation. Part way up leave at a gate/stile on the right, and a grassy path runs on the wallside beneath myriad hollies. Halfway along, bear left up a grassy way rising faintly to an old wall corner, then on behind a small building. A broader track then slants up through scattered trees to a gate at the top.

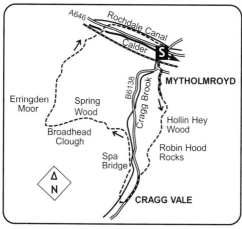

Don't go through, but take a path on the right for a grand walk along the top of Hollin Hey Wood. *Inspection lids marked 'MWW' indicate the line of an aqueduct constructed by Morley Water Works to supply the town from the reservoir it built at Withens Clough across Cragg Vale in 1894.* At the end the path emerges into more open country. *Revealed are outstanding views over Cragg Vale, with little urbanisation left to impinge. Finest features are the wealth of woodland, and the prospect of the wooded bowl of Broadhead Clough opposite, your return route.* The path advances to a seat above a rash of crags, a fine spot to halt. Just past here it dips down, and the main path slants down to the right. *Just ahead a thinner path continues onto the crest of Robin Hood Rocks.*

Your descending path quickly swings left, and avoiding lesser branches runs left to a stile out of the wood. Cross the field to the gateway ahead, but then turn down the nearside of the wall to a gate/stile. Continue on a clear path down by colourful vegetation to the edge of the wood, then bear left down a causeyed, walled way to a row of houses at Upper Birks in Cragg Vale. Turn down to the right here, and at the houses below drop left down onto the road. Go left on its footway past the Robin Hood pub. After further terraces bear right on a surfaced access road the very short way to Castlegate Mill, a pair of houses. Here take a path doubling back sharply right along the front, and running a firm course through trees it slants down onto a rough access road by Cragg Brook.

Cross the bridge to Papermill Cottage and from a gate on the right a broad path rises away, soon levelling out to run high above steep Papermill Wood. The left-hand wall soon disappears to leave you amid graceful beeches: within 75 yards fork right down towards the brook, and from a gate cross two narrow pastures to emerge onto a drive. Go down it to Spa Bridge, but without crossing take a stile to resume downstream on a permissive path. A lovely wooded walk leads to Clough Foot Bridge: just up to the left a gate/stile access a meadow, crossing it to resume downstream in woodland. The path soon swings left to a footbridge on a tiny brook, then rises onto a drive. *For an easy return, turn right down this to Dauber Bridge, from where the start is half a mile distant along the road.*

For part two of the walk, turn left up the drive rising alongside the wooded clough. At the end it forks: bear left on a good track running on to appraise the skyline of Broadhead Clough. Entering Spring Wood the drive forks: take neither, but go straight ahead along a much more inviting path. *Here you enter Yorkshire Wildlife Trust's Broadhead Clough Nature Reserve.* Initially flagged, the path winds on and gradually upwards into the deep confines of this glorious woodland. A flight of wooden steps leads to easier progress as a fence later comes in on the right. As the trees thin out to be replaced by bracken, the path crosses a stile in the fence, above which a surprise awaits as within a few feet it climbs to the rim of the amphitheatre, and the climbing is finished. A tall stake serves as a useful waymark for those locating the start of the path from above. *The great natural hollow of Broadhead Clough is also known locally as Bell Hole: this is truly a place to linger.*

Resume by crossing the few yards to a crumbling wall corner behind, and head off along a path down its long, scant length away across Erringden Moor. Evading some moist moments a wall corner is reached at the end. The path slants down to the left past an inner corner to another corner, then trace a faint trod bearing left across the corner of the moor, crossing quickly to a stile in a fence. Pass through the crumbling wall behind to start the long descent, the first section being alongside a long-abandoned hollowed way. *The valley floor quickly appears outspread below, with hillside settlements such as Midgley and Heptonstall prominent.* The old way leads down to a grassy cart track. Go right a few steps to a stile then resume the descent on a path slanting back to the left. *This proves a splendid route down through colourful open country.*

The path runs down towards a pylon, just beneath which it swings left towards the edge of trees. Along their fringe it turns downhill again, then slants right to a stile onto a drive, with a house just to the left. From a stile opposite, a thin path drops down by a wooded stream. Emerging just past another stile, continue down the fieldside to a single slab bridge at a tiny confluence. Now bear slightly left across the field to a gate in front of trees. A walled track is joined, and this leads down to the right. Bear left at the bottom, becoming surfaced to cross railway and river and emerge onto the main road alongside a tall, redundant mill. Cross the road with extreme caution to join the towpath of the Rochdale Canal (see page 49), and turn right for a short walk back into Mytholmroyd. Passing a lock and a couple of stone-arched bridges, leave the towpath at steps up to a modern road bridge. Turn right down Midgley Road, with the starting point just along to the right.

Descending into Cragg Vale from Hollin Hey Wood

OVENDEN MOOR

START Ogden   Grid ref. SE 066309

DISTANCE 5^{1}2 miles (9km)

ORDNANCE SURVEY MAPS
1:50,000
Landranger 104 - Leeds, Bradford & Harrogate
1:25,000
Explorer OL21 - South Pennines

ACCESS Start from the water company car park at Ogden Water, on Ogden Lane just off the A629 at Causeway Foot. Served by Halifax-Thornton-Bradford bus and Sunday Halifax-Denholme-Keighley bus.

Largely easy moorland walking from a popular reservoir

Ogden Reservoir was built in 1858, and now as Ogden Water offers woodland paths and an easy reservoir circuit. There is a visitor centre with refreshments and WCs between the car park and the dam. At the far end of the lower car park a kissing-gate sends a broad path off through the trees. Absorbing another, it angles very gently down towards the reservoir, meeting a lower, level path just short of the end. Near the head of the reservoir you reach a foot-bridge over a tiny side dam. While the reservoir circuit path crosses it, your way goes straight on, a thinner path that within a minute meets a broader one coming in from the right. Bear left on this, and ignoring an immediate left fork downhill, forge pleasantly on above the lively beck, rising ever gently.

Very quickly the end of the wood is reached, and a stile sends a path on through the open country of Ogden Clough. A degree of caution is needed where some small landslips have impinged on the route. Though an early fork drops down to a footbridge, you are quickly forced to re-cross the beck 'bridge-free', as the return bridge just ahead is inaccessible - perhaps better to remain on your bank where a well-used path skirts above the minor landslip here. *This steep-walled clough is a little gem, and the beckside path soon reaches twin waterfalls where the peaty moorland stream tumbles over uniform gritstone ledges.* At the second falls the path rises to a junction alongside a sturdy bridge over another little dam. *Immediately upstream are sizeable gritstone crags.* Across the waterworks bridge a path rises away to a stile onto the broad heather sweep of Ovenden Moor, and its wind turbines make their first appearance, looming alarmingly just ahead! A clear path heads away towards them, rising imperceptibly to a brow. *The wind turbines are now almost within touching distance, while just ahead the former Withens Hotel and two masts appear.*

The path drops to a waterworks bridge in Skirden Clough, then rises as a broader track to meet the firm track of Withens New Road. For a quick return go left here, otherwise turn right for two minutes to the road alongside The Withens. *Up to the 21st century this was the Withens Hotel, built in 1862 to serve quarrymen, and until its closure*

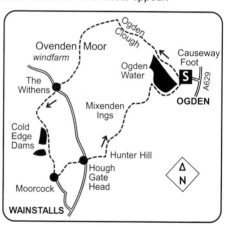

the highest pub in West Yorkshire. Five minutes along the road leads to an information area at the windfarm, operational since 1993. You will discover that these 23 wind turbines are 100ft high and can power 5,600 homes: slightly suspicious that on a previous visit this figure was quoted as 7,500? Try to calculate how many would be needed to supply Calderdale: you'd certainly need an alternative activity to rambling anyway, because there wouldn't be any room left on the moors for you and me!

To resume, cross straight over Cold Edge Road and down a walled cart-track. This swings left then down to the right to ruinous farm buildings. Passing to their right it runs along towards the restored Haighcote Barn. Again passing right, its rough access road is joined to swing left to approach the Cold Edge Dams. Just short of the first one, Haigh Cote Dam, branch off to join a thin path along the embankment. *This is the home of Halifax Water Ski Club, with a little clubhouse, slipway and jetty.* Follow this to the far end of the main embankment. The path then crosses a little tract of heather moorland to do likewise on the smaller Leadbeater Dam. At the first corner, however, turn down a path across further moorland towards a clump of trees, passing to their right. Instead of going left to a fence, a thinner path goes straight ahead to locate a corner stile below, admitting onto the rough road left earlier. Go right for two minutes, absorbing the Calderdale Way for the next half-mile through the fields.

Immediately after the first buildings on the left turn into the yard at Moorcock Farm. *The main building is unrecognisable as the isolated Moorcock pub this was until as recently as 2002.* At the far corner enter a field, crossing its centre to the next stile. A narrow, enclosed path heads away beneath a small dam, then along a flagged fieldside onto another walled rough road opposite some houses. Go left a few strides, then from a stile on the right cross straight over the field to a plank footbridge. Ascend the wallside behind, and part way up cross a stile to resume up the other side of a fence. Over a stile at the top the path goes round to the left of Hough Gate Head Farm, and up a track to join its drive just before joining Cold Edge Road.

Once again go left a few strides, then from a kissing-gate on the right a grassy, part-flagged track heads away. After a spell between walls it swings gently right, descending steadily into a quarried area at Hunter Hill. *Ahead is a sweeping prospect over the northern Halifax suburbs.* The Calderdale Way heads into the heart of this varied scene, but you must part company. At a crossroads of tracks the Way prepares to become enclosed again: here take the inviting branch left towards four sycamores. The low ruins in their shadow are all that remains of Slaughter Gap. *This was named after a Civil War skirmish in 1644, when Parliamentarian troops came off worst.* After the last ruin a thin trod contours across to a kissing-gate at a wall junction back onto a grassy corner of Ovenden Moor. Follow the wall away until it turns off, then a fence shadows the thin path to the edge of a steeper slope. Halifax golf club is outspread, occupying a colourful hollow that would look nicer still in its natural condition. The path descends pleasantly to a stile onto the course. A bell lets you warn anyone teeing off to your right of your presence, as you cross straight over a fairway, then bear gently left on a track, over a cross-tracks to a bridge over the central stream.

Just a short way further, alongside a green, a path scales the slope alongside a patch of bracken, slanting right as you gain height along the bracken fringe. On the brow, head straight across another fairway to rejoin Withens New Road in front of a plantation. While the track leads quickly down to the dam, a nicer finish takes the stile in front. A broad path runs down through the trees towards the reservoir wall, ignoring lesser branches. When it swings left to climb away, take a stile in the wall just to your right to join the reservoir path. Turn right along here to the dam, then cross it to conclude. Perhaps inevitably in view of their familiarity, the wind turbines make a final appearance on crossing the dam.

In Ogden Clough

LUDDENDEN DEAN

START Booth   Grid ref. SE 036277

DISTANCE 5¹⁄2 miles (9km)

ORDNANCE SURVEY MAPS
1:50,000
Landranger 104 - Leeds, Bradford & Harrogate
1:25,000
Explorer OL21 - South Pennines

ACCESS Start from Jerusalem Farm near Luddenden, car park half a mile west of Booth Village on Jerusalem Lane. Booth is served by bus from Halifax/Sowerby Bridge via Luddenden Foot.

> Absorbing rambling in and around a relatively unsung side valley with a wealth of interesting features and old houses

Jerusalem Farm is run by Calderdale Countryside Service, with environmental workshops, school visits and a campsite. From the entrance turn back down the road towards Booth. Beyond the trees, almost hidden on the left is a stile. From it slant down a wallside onto the main road through Booth. *Opposite is the former Independent Sabbath School of 1850.* Cross straight over and down steps and cobbles, past a graveyard to a lower road at rows of houses at Goit Side. *One of these was a Friends' Meeting House of 1770.* Turn right to a cobbled fork at two characterful houses. Bear left, then keep straight on the broad track.

This runs on to two final houses, from where the bridleway continues on into trees. Very soon it emerges at another row of houses, Brook Terrace. At the end the access road goes left over the brook, but your way is straight on, and beyond some setts it narrows back to a bridleway. It runs a firm course in the company of Luddenden Brook to fork just short of Luddenden village. Either takes you into the centre, the left one going via the church. *This charming village oozes with character, with pub and church at the heart of things. The Lord Nelson is an attractive place sporting a 1634 datestone: Branwell Bronte drank here when employed as ticket clerk at Luddenden Foot railway station. Just across the tiny square a war memorial stands in front of St Mary's church of 1816.*

Turn down to the left and over the bridge to High Street Fold. Here take a cobbled path on the right, running downstream to a footbridge. Don't cross but take steps on the left to rise darkly onto a road. *Alongside is a millstone where an ancient cornmill stood.* Cross at this junction to a sloping green. *This features a rope drum from a local mill closed in 1982.* Here take the first drive on the right, quickly becoming a briefly enclosed path emerging into new housing on the site of a mill. Keep straight on, the path returning near the end to head off into trees.

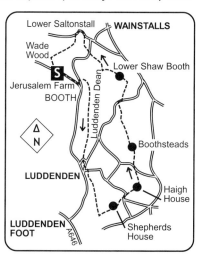

Below is the brook again, and in between is a long dry former mill-cut. A fork is quickly reached. *The right branch makes a two-minute detour over the mill-cut to an attractive, narrow arched footbridge almost lost in undergrowth.* Your route takes the upper branch, curving round past a gritstone outcrop to a crossroads of paths beneath a flight of stone steps. Turn up these to a stile up into a field. Cross to a gate opposite, then on to the top corner beneath the house at Roebucks. From a corner stile turn up the fieldside to a gate/stile above the house and up the drive. *Before leaving note the unconventional arrangement of this unsung gem dating from 1633.*

At once a junction is reached: while the drive goes right, you turn up the walled way to the left. *Over to the left is Luddenden*

Foot, a suburban sprawl that long since passed Luddenden in size though not in character: note historic Kershaw House surviving amongst incongruous modern development. Beyond, the Calder Valley and Luddenden Dean are divided by Midgley Moor, while Ovenden Moor windfarm rises over the moors at your dalehead. Just below you, note the interesting roof arrangement at Roebucks. The improving grassy way levels out to approach the first of several houses at Shepherds House. Keep straight on the drive, rising to join a road on a hairpin bend. Go left down to the next bend, then take a narrow stone stairway up into the wood, just left of a path by the tiny stream. When the steps end the path runs to the right, soon ascending a second flight to slant right to a stile at the wood top. Go straight up the field, over an old green way and ladder-stile and up a crumbling wallside towards Haigh House. *Though largely hidden this is another fine old house, dating from 1631 and with yet more mullioned windows.*

A stile at the top sends an enclosed path rising left of the buildings to a stile by the driveway at the field top: don't use it but go left on the field top to emerge via a stile onto an ascending road. *Luddenden Dean increasingly takes the interest as you forge deeper into it from this contouring route across its eastern flank.* Cross straight over and along the drive opposite, which ends at 18th century Boothsteads Farm. From a gateway on the left just before the house, advance past the buildings on a rough track through the yard. From a gate into the field at the back head directly away with a wall on the right. After a gateway head on again, and though the map suggests crossing the wall at a tiny kink further on, in the absence of a stile it is better to keep on to a gate just short of the end, and continue to a stile onto an enclosed grassy track. From a stile opposite resume with a right-hand wall to a stile onto an old green way: turn down its overgrown course onto a road.

Go right past houses, and after a small enclosure take a stile on the left. Turn down the wallside, but on reaching a vestige of a wall above a steeper drop, turn right with it. *The views into the finest section of Luddenden Dean are superb.* At the end cross a stile and continue beneath a wall on the top of the scrubby bank to join an old grassy way beneath a cylindrical air shaft. Go left along here to Lower Shaw Booth. *Yet another splendid old house about 300 years old, in this curious arrangement the central part is the most interesting, with an incredible array of mullioned windows strung along the ground floor.* Go straight ahead between the houses into a field. Bear left down the wallside, through a bridle-gate at the corner and on a thin path towards a house. A gate just above puts you onto a hairpin bend of a drive. Turn up to the next such bend, then go straight ahead over a big stone stile.

A gem of an embanked little path runs on through several small fields to a house at Peace Cote. *Ahead, note the little settlement of Lower Saltonstall on the slope in front, an ancient cluster of dark, low houses at one with their surroundings.* From a gate onto the drive by the house go straight over to a stile, and a little path slants down to a road. Again go straight over to a stile, then down a thin wallside path to the house at Hock Cliff. Pass to its right and head away along a cart track. At the road go left to Catywell Bridge and the sudden appearance of the hitherto hidden Cat-i-the-Well pub. *Tucked away on a dead-end road, this enduring watering hole is a corruption of Caty Well, found on the roadside just above the pub.* Continue on from the pub for a minute only to Lower Saltonstall. *This hamlet was a vaccary (cattle farm) run by the Manor of Wakefield 700 years ago.*

After the first house on the left turn down a short access track, passing between the houses and down to a gate into a field. Head down the wallside as far as a gate/stile in it, then trace the field-top wall to the next stile. Bear half-left to a gate/stile opposite, from where a faint old made path goes diagonally across to a wall-stile. Behind, a little gate admits into the top of Wade Wood. *This superb deciduous wood comprises largely of birch, oak, beech, holly and much colourful vegetation.* A thin path slants down to the right, with steps down to a cross-paths. *This is a junction with an ancient track from Saltonstall towards Midgley.* Keep straight on down the path ahead to Wade Bridge. *This dates back to the early 19th century, and was rebuilt after flood damage. Its width shows it was meant for the passage of carts rather than mere pedestrian and equestrian use. This charming corner is a place to linger as Luddenden Brook meanders over its stony bed, and the end is just two minutes away!* Cross the bridge and go left up the enclosed green way to return to Jerusalem.

MIDGLEY MOOR

START *Booth   Grid ref. SE 036277*

DISTANCE *6 miles (9^{1}2km)*

ORDNANCE SURVEY MAPS
1:50,000
Landranger 104 - Leeds, Bradford & Harrogate
1:25,000
Explorer OL21 - South Pennines

ACCESS *Start from Jerusalem Farm near Luddenden, car park half a mile west of Booth Village on Jerusalem Lane. Booth is served by bus from Halifax/Sowerby Bridge via Luddenden Foot.*

A breezy encounter with heather moorland and a simple stroll down a well-wooded valley: excellent views

Jerusalem Farm is run by Calderdale Countryside Service, with environmental workshops, school visits and campsite. Rejoin the road and drop a few strides to a stile opposite. A good path slants left up a colourful bank to a big wall-stile. *Already you enjoy big views over Luddenden Dean.* A little path maintains this slant up another steep pasture to the top corner. From the stile go left on the wallside, curving up to a gate into the cobbled yard at some houses. Follow the drive out to a road, noting a neat short-cut on the right just before the end. Go a few strides right to a small gate beneath the row of houses at Green House, and cross to the garden top where a gate puts you into a field. Ascend directly up the wall-side, into a planted enclosure and then up the outside of a garden at Height Farm with a fence leading to a wall-stile at the top.

This puts you onto the lovely heather of Midgley Moor, and just in front an excellent path runs left above the wall. When a fence takes over remain on the moor, the wall soon returning on a bend.

From here you look down on Luddenden Foot in the main valley, and more impressively to Cragg Vale, Broadhead Clough and Stoodley Pike. The path leads delightfully on above a lone house until the wall ultimately drops away: here the path bears gently right to begin a steady rise above old quarries to reach a wall corner, with the standing stone of Churn Milk Joan a minute higher at a path junction. *This sturdy six-footer may have been a medieval cross, and its hollowed top still sees the leaving of 'alms' for the needy.* Turn left here on a level path merging with the wall. When the wall turns sharply off again, the path strikes gently left across the moor, incorporating a flagged section to reach a stile in a fence ahead. It now drops a little towards Hebden Bridge golf clubhouse. *Here you earn a sudden view up-dale over Hebden Bridge and Heptonstall.* Remaining on the moor the wide path contours round to the right above the course and below old quarries in a great loop under Cock Hill. After the course a way comes up from the left and you simply continue on through a gate/stile, very gently rising with the intake wall or replacement fence. *The village of Old Town is just below.*

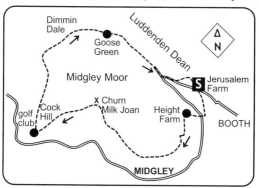

A good path now takes you along the moor bottom beneath insignificant Sheep Stones Edge. The path is only vacated when it turns sharp left with the wall. Instead turn right on a thinner path heading gently up the grassy moor. After a short climb it levels out on the broad ridge where it crosses a broader path. Advance straight on, briefly a little moistly in parts, past remains of stone shooting butts in the depression known as Dimmin Dale. *Luddenden*

Dean appears with Ovenden Moor windfarm on its skyline. The path soon drops towards the Luddenden side of the moor, meeting another path coming in from the left to bear right to a crumbling wall corner at the well-defined moor edge. *Now enjoy superb views into Luddenden Dean, with the reservoirs visible up the valley.* While a path runs along the edge to the right, yours begins to descend, doubling back briefly to the old wall. *Note the ruin of Castle Carr's old gatehouse in the trees up-dale. Castle Carr was a massive Victorian castle surrounded by ornamental gardens. Later abandoned, it fell into neglect and was finally dismantled in 1961. Down below, meanwhile, is the lower lodge.*

The path enjoys a well-graded slant down to the right, and leaves the moor at a gate just above Goose Green. A splendid green way winds down between walls onto the enclosed track of Wood Lane by a nice house. Turn right on this for a grand short mile, becoming fully surfaced to rise to a junction with a hairpin bend. Go left to return to Jerusalem Farm. For a nicer finish, part way down take a stile into the start of Wade Wood, and a path slants down beneath graceful beeches to a stile, just beneath which it drops to Wade Bridge on Luddenden Brook. *This dates back to the early 19th century, and was rebuilt after flood damage. Its width shows it was meant for the passage of carts rather than mere pedestrian and equestrian use. This charming corner is a place to linger as Luddenden Brook meanders over its stony bed, and the end is just two minutes away!* Don't cross but slant right up the enclosed green way to return to Jerusalem.

Churn Milk Joan, Midgley Moor

WALK LOG

WALK	DATE	NOTES
1		
2		
3		
4		
5		
6		
7		
8		
9		
10		
11		
12		
13		
14		
15		
16		
17		
18		
19		
20		
21		
22		
23		
24		
25		

INDEX
walk number refers